61st Annual Meeting of the Association for Computational Linguistics (ACL 2023)

Tutorial Abstracts

Toronto, Canada
9 July 2023

ISBN: 978-1-7138-8178-0

Printed from e-media with permission by:

Curran Associates, Inc.
57 Morehouse Lane
Red Hook, NY 12571

CURRAN ASSOCIATES INC.
proceedings.com

Some format issues inherent in the e-media version may also appear in this print version.

Printed with permission by Curran Associates, Inc. (2024)

For permission requests, please contact the Association for Computational Linguistics
at the address below.

Association for Computational Linguistics
209 N. Eighth Street
Stroudsburg, Pennsylvania 18360

Phone: 1-570-476-8006
Fax: 1-570-476-0860

acl@aclweb.org

Additional copies of this publication are available from:

Curran Associates, Inc.
57 Morehouse Lane
Red Hook, NY 12571 USA
Phone: 845-758-0400
Fax: 845-758-2633
Email: curran@proceedings.com
Web: www.proceedings.com

ACL 2023

The 61st Annual Meeting of the Association for Computational Linguistics: Tutorial Abstracts

Proceedings of the Tutorial Abstracts

July 9, 2023

Order copies of this and other ACL proceedings from:

Association for Computational Linguistics (ACL)
209 N. Eighth Street
Stroudsburg, PA 18360
USA
Tel: +1-570-476-8006
Fax: +1-570-476-0860
acl@aclweb.org

Introduction

Welcome to the Tutorials Session of ACL 2023.

The ACL tutorials session is organized to give conference attendees a comprehensive introduction by expert researchers to some topics of importance drawn from our rapidly growing and changing research field.

This year, as has been the tradition over the past few years, the call, submission, reviewing and selection of tutorials were coordinated jointly for multiple conferences: EACL, ACL, and EMNLP. We formed a review committee including the EACL tutorial chairs (Sameer Pradhan and Fabio Massimo Zanzotto) and ACL tutorial chairs (Yun-Nung Vivian Chen, Margot Mieskes, and Siva Reddy). A reviewing process was organized so that each proposal receives 2 reviews. The selection criteria included clarity, preparedness, novelty, timeliness, instructors' experience, likely audience, open access to the teaching materials, diversity (multilingualism, gender, age and geolocation) and the compatibility of preferred venues. A total of 42 tutorial submissions were received, of which 6 were selected for presentation at ACL.

We would like to thank the tutorial authors for their contributions and flexibility while organising the conference in a hybrid format. Finally, our thanks go to the conference organizers for effective collaboration, and in particular to the general chair Yang Liu.

We hope you enjoy the tutorials.

ACL 2023 Tutorial Co-chairs
Yun-Nung (Vivian) Chen
Margot Mieskes
Siva Reddy

Organizing Committee

General Chair

Yang Liu, Amazon, USA

Program Chairs

Jordan Boyd-Graber, University of Maryland, USA
Naoaki Okazaki, Tokyo Institute of Technology, Japan
Anna Rogers, IT University of Copenhagen, Denmark

Tutorial Chairs

Yun-Nung (Vivian) Chen, National Taiwan University, Taiwan
Margot Margot, University of Applied Sciences, Darmstadt, Germany
Siva Reddy, McGill University and Mila, Canada

Table of Contents

Goal Awareness for Conversational AI: Proactivity, Non-collaborativity, and Beyond

Yang Deng[1], **Wenqiang Lei**[2], **Minlie Huang**[3], **Tat-Seng Chua**[4]
[1] The Chinese University of Hong Kong [2]Sichuan University
[3] Tsinghua University [4] National University of Singapore
ydeng@se.cuhk.edu.hk wenqianglei@gmail.com
aihuang@tsinghua.edu.cn chuats@comp.nus.edu.sg

1 Introduction

Tutorial Description Conversational systems are envisioned to provide social support or functional service to human users via natural language interactions. Conventional conversation researches mainly focus on the response-ability of the system, such as dialogue context understanding and response generation, but overlooks the design of an essential property in intelligent conversations, *i.e.*, goal awareness. The awareness of goals means the state of not only being responsive to the users but also aware of the target conversational goal and capable of leading the conversation towards the goal, which is a significant step towards higher-level intelligence and artificial consciousness. It can not only largely improve user engagement and service efficiency in the conversation, but also empower the system to handle more complicated conversation tasks that involve strategical and motivational interactions. In this tutorial, we will introduce the recent advances on the design of agent's awareness of goals in a wide range of conversational systems.
Type of Tutorial Cutting-edge
Targeted Audience Target audiences are researchers and practitioners who interested in natural language processing and human-computer interaction. The audience will learn about the state-of-the-art research in conversational AI and the cutting-edge designs of agent's awareness in various conversational systems.
Suggested Duration Half day (3 hours)

2 Tutorial Outline

Part I: Preliminary (20 minutes)

Conversational agents are generally envisioned to achieve the conversational goal by providing social support or functional service to human users via natural language interactions. In terms of the goal, Part I will present a brief overview of the widely-studied problems and correponding mainstream approaches in several typical conversational systems, including open-domain dialogue (ODD) systems (Zhang et al., 2018a; Li et al., 2017; Roller et al., 2021), task-oriented dialogue (TOD) systems (Budzianowski et al., 2018; Lei et al., 2018; Su et al., 2022), conversational question answering (CQA) systems (Choi et al., 2018; Reddy et al., 2019; Anantha et al., 2021; Qiu et al., 2021), and conversational recommender systems (CRS) (Li et al., 2018; Deng et al., 2021; Wang et al., 2022).

Part II: Proactive Conversational Systems (50 minutes)

As opposed to responding to users, proactivity is the most prominent feature of goal awareness in conversational systems, which can improve the collaboration between the users and system towards the ultimate conversation goal. Derived from the definition of proactivity in organizational behaviors (Grant and Ashford, 2008) and its dictionary definitions (Dictionary, 1989), conversational agents' proactivity can be defined as the capability to create or control the conversation by taking the initiative and anticipating impacts on themselves or human users. In this part, we will provide a comprehensive introduction about such efforts on the design of agent's proactivity that span various task formulations and application scenarios. In specific, we categorize them in three directions according to the application scenario, and plan to discuss their research problems and methods as follows:

- **Topic Shifting and Planning in Open-domain Dialogues** The goal of OOD systems is to maintain engaging social conversations with users. Proactive OOD systems can consciously change topics (Rachna et al., 2021; Xie et al., 2021) and lead directions (Tang et al., 2019; Wu et al., 2019; Yang et al., 2022) for improving user engagement in the conversation. We will present the existing methods for topic shifting and planning in open-domain dialogues, including graph-based topic

Proceedings of the 61st Annual Meeting of the Association for Computational Linguistics
Volume 6: Tutorial Abstracts, pages 1–10
July 9, 2023 ©2023 Association for Computational Linguistics

planning (Qin et al., 2020; Zhong et al., 2021; Xu et al., 2020; Ni et al., 2022), responding plan generation (Kishinami et al., 2022), and learning from interactions with users (Lei et al., 2022).

- **Additional Information Delivery in Task-oriented Dialogues** The goal of TOD systems is to provide functional service for users, such as making reservations or managing schedule. The proactivity in TOD systems is firstly defined as the capability of consciously providing additional information that is not requested by but useful to the users (Balaraman and Magnini, 2020a,b), which can improve the quality and effectiveness of conveying functional service in the conversation. We will introduce the recent studies of proactive TOD systems with various designs. For instance, Sun et al. (2021) add topical chit-chats into the responses for TODs. Chen et al. (2022c) enrich task-oriented dialogues with relevant entity knowledge.
- **Uncertainty Elimination in Information-seeking Dialogues** The goal of CIS systems (Zamani et al., 2022) is to fulfill the user's information needs and its typical applications include conversational search, conversational recommendation, and conversational question answering. Conventional CIS systems assume that users always convey clear information requests, while the user queries, in reality, are often brief and succinct. Recent years have witnessed several advances on developing proactive CIS systems that can consciously eliminate the uncertainty for more efficient and precise information seeks by initiating a subdialogue. Such a subdialogue can either clarify the ambiguity of the query or question in conversational search (Aliannejadi et al., 2019, 2021; Zamani et al., 2020) and conversation question answering (Guo et al., 2021; Deng et al., 2022a), or elicit the user preference in conversational recommendation (Zhang et al., 2018b; Lei et al., 2020a,b).

Part III: Non-collaborative Conversational Systems (40 minutes)

Most of existing conversational systems are built upon the assumption that the users willingly collaborate with the conversational agent to reach the mutual goal. However, this assumption may not always hold in some real-world scenarios, where the users and the system do not share the same goal (He et al., 2018; Wang et al., 2019) or the users are not willing to coordinate with the agent (Yang et al., 2019; Kim et al., 2022). In these cases, the conversational agent requires another feature of goal awareness, *i.e.*, non-collaborativity (Li et al., 2020; Zhou et al., 2020), which means the capability of handling both in-goal and off-goal dialogues appropriately for ultimately leading back to the system's goal. In this part, we will categorize the non-collaborative settings into two groups as follows and cover their to-date work respectively.

- **The users and the system do not share the same goal.** Typical applications include persuasion dialogues (Wang et al., 2019), negotiation dialogues (He et al., 2018; Chawla et al., 2021), and anti-scam dialogues (Li et al., 2020). We will present the approaches for the system to consciously mitigate and resolve the conflict goals with users, including dialogue strategy learning (Dutt et al., 2021; Yamaguchi et al., 2021; Joshi et al., 2021), user personality modeling (Shi et al., 2021; Yang et al., 2021), and response style transfer (Mishra et al., 2022; Wu et al., 2021).
- **The users are not willing to coordinate with the agent.** Example scenarios include calming down the emotional users before solving their problems (Liu et al., 2021b), managing the users' complaints before providing service (Yang et al., 2019), and handling problematic content during the conversations (Kim et al., 2022). We will introduce the pioneering studies for the system to consciously deal with non-collaborative users during the conversation, including emotion cause analysis (Tu et al., 2022; Cheng et al., 2022), user satisfaction estimation (Liu et al., 2021a; Deng et al., 2022b), and safe response generation (Baheti et al., 2021; Ung et al., 2022).

Part IV: Multi-goal Conversational Systems (30 minutes)

All the aforementioned conversational systems assume that users always know what they want and the system solely targets at reaching a certain goal, such as chit-chat, question answering, recommendation, etc. The system with a higher level of agent's awareness of goals should also be capable of handling conversations with multiple and various goals. As for multi-goal conversational systems (Liu et al., 2022; Deng et al., 2022c), the agent is expected to consciously discover users' intentions and naturally lead user-engaged dialogues with multiple conversation goals. We will cover the newly proposed problems in multi-goal conversational systems with their corresponding data resources (Sun et al., 2021; Zhao et al., 2022; Young et al., 2022; Chiu et al., 2022). Then we will discuss two problem settings of multi-goal conversational systems with corresponding state-of-the-art approaches: (i) The goal sequence is pre-defined (Bai et al., 2021; Zhang et al., 2021b), and (ii) The next goal needs to be predicted (Liu et al., 2020; Chen et al., 2022b; Deng et al., 2022c).

Part V: Open Challenges for Conversational Agents' Awareness and Beyond (40 minutes)

In the last part, we will discuss the main open challenges in developing agent's awareness in conversational systems and several potential research directions for future studies.

- **Evaluation for Conversational Agent's Awareness** The development of robust evaluation protocols has already been a long-standing problem for different kinds of conversational systems (Zhang et al., 2021a; Peng et al., 2021; Li et al., 2022b). The evaluation for conversational agent's awareness is a more challenging problem, since it is involved the evaluation not only from the perspective of natural language, but also from the perspectives of human-computer interaction, sociology, psychology, etc. We will cover the latest studies for shedding some lights on this topic, inclusive of popular metrics such as goal completion and user satisfaction (Liu et al., 2020; Lei et al., 2022; Gupta et al., 2022), and model-based methods such as user simulator (Zhang and Balog, 2020; Sekulic et al., 2022).

- **Ethics for Conversational Agent's Awareness** Although existing designs of agent's awareness of goals in conversational systems generally aim at social goodness (Wang et al., 2019; Liu et al., 2021b; Kim et al., 2022), it is inevitably a double-edged sword that can be used for good or evil. For responsible NLP researches, we will discuss several important aspects of ethical issues in conscious conversational systems: (i) Factuality: Factual incorrectness and hallucination of knowledge are common in conversational systems (Dziri et al., 2022; Honovich et al., 2021). When enabling the conversational agent with awareness, it becomes more crucial to guarantee the factuality of the system-provided information (Chen et al., 2022a). (ii) Safety: Besides general dialogue safety problems, such as toxic language and social bias (Saveski et al., 2021; Barikeri et al., 2021), conscious conversational systems need to pay more attentions to the aggressiveness issue during the non-collaborative conversations (Kim et al., 2022; Hu et al., 2022). (iii) Privacy: The privacy issue is overlooked in current studies on conversational systems (Li et al., 2022a; Shi et al., 2022), but the agent's awareness raises concerns about how these conversational systems handle personal information obtained from the users. Furthermore, we will introduce some recent released resources that can be adopted for studying this topic (Ziems et al., 2022; Sun et al., 2022; Kim et al., 2022).

- **Agent's Awareness in LLM-based Conversational AI** Large Language Models (LLMs) have been demonstrated to be powerful of handling various NLP tasks in the form of conversations, such as ChatGPT (Schulman et al., 2022), LaMDA (Thoppilan et al., 2022), BlenderBot (Shuster et al., 2022), etc. However, these applications are typically designed to follow the user's instructions and intents. There are still several limitations that attribute to the lack of agent's awareness, such as passively providing randomly-guessed answers to ambiguous user queries, failing to refuse or handle problematic user requests that may exhibit harmful or biased conversations, etc. In addition, they also fall short of interacting under non-collaborative or system-oriented settings. Therefore, we will discuss the role of LLMs in goal awareness for conversational AI with some latest studies (Huang et al., 2022; Ahn et al., 2022; Yao et al., 2022).

3 Presenters

Yang Deng is a final-year Ph.D. candidate in The Chinese University of Hong Kong. His research lies in natural language processing and information retrieval, especially for dialogue and QA systems. He has published over 20 papers at top venues such as ACL, EMNLP, SIGIR, WWW, TKDE, and TOIS. Additional information is available at `https://dengyang17.github.io`.

Wenqiang Lei is a Professor in Sichuan University. His research interests focus on conversational AI, including conversational recommendation, dialogue and QA systems. He has published relevant papers at top venues such as ACL, EMNLP, KDD, SIGIR, TOIS, and received the ACM MM

2020 best paper award. He has given tutorials on the topic of conversational recommendation at RecSys 2021, SIGIR 2020, and co-organized special issues about conversational information seeking on ACM Trans. on Web. Specifically, his tutorial on SIGIR 2020 accepts over 1600 audiences, being one of the most popular tutorials in SIGIR 2020. Additional information is available at `https://sites.google.com/view/wenqianghome/home`.

Minlie Huang is an Associate Professor with the Department of Computer Science and Technology, Tsinghua University. He has authored or coauthored more than 100 papers in premier conferences and journals (ACL, EMNLP, TACL, etc). His research interests include natural language processing, particularly in dialog systems, reading comprehension, and sentiment analysis. He is an editor of TACL, CL, TNNLS, the Area Chair or SAC of ACL/EMNLP for more than 10 times. He is the recipient of IJCAI 2018 distinguished paper award, a nominee of ACL 2019 best demo papers, and SIGDIAL 2020 best paper award. Additional information is available at `http://coai.cs.tsinghua.edu.cn/hml`.

Tat-Seng Chua is the KITHCT Chair Professor with the School of Computing, National University of Singapore. His main research interest include multimedia information retrieval and social media analytics. He is the 2015 winner of the prestigious ACM SIGMM Technical Achievement Award and receives the best papers (or candidates) over 10 times in top conferences (SIGIR, WWW, MM, etc). He serves as the general co-chair of top conferences multiple times (MM 2005, SIGIR 2008, WSDM 2023, etc), and the editors of multiple journals (TOIS, TMM, etc). He has given invited keynote talks at multiple top conferences, including the recent one on the topic of multimodal conversational search and recommendation. Additional information is available at `https://www.chuatatseng.com/`.

4 Reading Lists

Previous Tutorials:
(Chen et al., 2017b) ACL 2017 - Deep Learning for Dialogue Systems;
(Su et al., 2018) NAACL 2018 - Deep Learning for Conversational AI;
(Gao et al., 2018) ACL 2018/SIGIR 2018 - Neural Approaches to Conversational AI;
(Gao et al., 2020) SIGIR 2020 - Recent Advances in Conversational Information Retrieval;
(Dalton et al., 2022) SIGIR 2022 - Conversational Information Seeking: Theory and Application.

Related Surveys or Book Chapters:
(Chen et al., 2017a) A Survey on Dialogue Systems: Recent Advances and New Frontiers;
(Gao et al., 2019) Neural Approaches to Conversational AI;
(Huang et al., 2020) Challenges in Building Intelligent Open-domain Dialog Systems;
(Zamani et al., 2022) Conversational Information Seeking;
(Gao et al., 2022) Neural Approaches to Conversational Information Retrieval;
(Yan et al., 2022) Deep Learning for Dialogue Systems: Chit-Chat and Beyond.

5 Other Tutorial Information

Breadth and Diversity Considerations According to the representative set of papers listed in the selected bibliography, the concerned work in this tutorial will contain only 10%-15% of work that involves at least one of the four presenters. The rest of the tutorial will present a comprehensive overview of the tutorial topic by discussing the related work as much as possible from other researchers. The discussed approaches are problem-driven and language-agnostic, which means that the introduced content are generally applicable to all languages. The techniques are also not limited to a certain type of dialogues and can be generalized to diverse conversational systems. We have a diverse background for the presenters across multiple institutions in different regions.

Ethical Considerations Artificial consciousness is a broad and essential topic towards "Strong AI" in the whole AI community (Searle, 1992), which can and should be used for social goodness, but inevitably comes with potential risks. In fact, the awareness of goals is just one of the cognitive aspects of consciousness (Baars, 1993). As part of this tutorial, we will provide a specific section for discussing the ethical considerations and designs for agent's awareness in conversational systems. This tutorial also provides the opportunity to arouse discussions on how far we can and should go for agent's consciousness in conversational AI from the view of ethical and responsible NLP researches.

Open Access of Materials All tutorial materials will be made publicly available.

References

Michael Ahn, Anthony Brohan, Noah Brown, Yevgen Chebotar, Omar Cortes, Byron David, Chelsea Finn, Keerthana Gopalakrishnan, Karol Hausman, Alexander Herzog, Daniel Ho, Jasmine Hsu, Julian Ibarz, Brian Ichter, Alex Irpan, Eric Jang, Rosario Jauregui Ruano, Kyle Jeffrey, Sally Jesmonth, Nikhil J. Joshi, Ryan Julian, Dmitry Kalashnikov, Yuheng Kuang, Kuang-Huei Lee, Sergey Levine, Yao Lu, Linda Luu, Carolina Parada, Peter Pastor, Jornell Quiambao, Kanishka Rao, Jarek Rettinghouse, Diego Reyes, Pierre Sermanet, Nicolas Sievers, Clayton Tan, Alexander Toshev, Vincent Vanhoucke, Fei Xia, Ted Xiao, Peng Xu, Sichun Xu, and Mengyuan Yan. 2022. Do as I can, not as I say: Grounding language in robotic affordances. *CoRR*, abs/2204.01691.

Mohammad Aliannejadi, Julia Kiseleva, Aleksandr Chuklin, Jeff Dalton, and Mikhail S. Burtsev. 2021. Building and evaluating open-domain dialogue corpora with clarifying questions. In *EMNLP 2021*, pages 4473–4484.

Mohammad Aliannejadi, Hamed Zamani, Fabio Crestani, and W. Bruce Croft. 2019. Asking clarifying questions in open-domain information-seeking conversations. In *SIGIR 2019*, pages 475–484.

Raviteja Anantha, Svitlana Vakulenko, Zhucheng Tu, Shayne Longpre, Stephen Pulman, and Srinivas Chappidi. 2021. Open-domain question answering goes conversational via question rewriting. In *Proceedings of the 2021 Conference of the North American Chapter of the Association for Computational Linguistics: Human Language Technologies, NAACL-HLT 2021*, pages 520–534.

Bernard J Baars. 1993. *A cognitive theory of consciousness*. Cambridge University Press.

Ashutosh Baheti, Maarten Sap, Alan Ritter, and Mark O. Riedl. 2021. Just say no: Analyzing the stance of neural dialogue generation in offensive contexts. In *Proceedings of the 2021 Conference on Empirical Methods in Natural Language Processing, EMNLP 2021*, pages 4846–4862.

Jiaqi Bai, Ze Yang, Xinnian Liang, Wei Wang, and Zhoujun Li. 2021. Learning to copy coherent knowledge for response generation. In *Thirty-Fifth AAAI Conference on Artificial Intelligence, AAAI 2021*, pages 12535–12543.

Vevake Balaraman and Bernardo Magnini. 2020a. Investigating proactivity in task-oriented dialogues. In *Proceedings of the Seventh Italian Conference on Computational Linguistics, CLiC-it 2020*, volume 2769.

Vevake Balaraman and Bernardo Magnini. 2020b. Proactive systems and influenceable users: Simulating proactivity in task-oriented dialogues. In *Proc. 24th Workshop Semantics Pragmatics Dialogue (SEMDIAL)*, pages 1–12.

Soumya Barikeri, Anne Lauscher, Ivan Vulic, and Goran Glavas. 2021. Redditbias: A real-world resource for bias evaluation and debiasing of conversational language models. In *Proceedings of the 59th Annual Meeting of the Association for Computational Linguistics and the 11th International Joint Conference on Natural Language Processing, ACL/IJCNLP 2021*, pages 1941–1955.

Pawel Budzianowski, Tsung-Hsien Wen, Bo-Hsiang Tseng, Iñigo Casanueva, Stefan Ultes, Osman Ramadan, and Milica Gasic. 2018. Multiwoz - A large-scale multi-domain wizard-of-oz dataset for task-oriented dialogue modelling. In *Proceedings of the 2018 Conference on Empirical Methods in Natural Language Processing*, pages 5016–5026.

Kushal Chawla, Jaysa Ramirez, Rene Clever, Gale M. Lucas, Jonathan May, and Jonathan Gratch. 2021. Casino: A corpus of campsite negotiation dialogues for automatic negotiation systems. In *Proceedings of the 2021 Conference of the North American Chapter of the Association for Computational Linguistics: Human Language Technologies, NAACL-HLT 2021*, pages 3167–3185.

Hongshen Chen, Xiaorui Liu, Dawei Yin, and Jiliang Tang. 2017a. A survey on dialogue systems: Recent advances and new frontiers. *SIGKDD Explor.*, 19(2):25–35.

Maximillian Chen, Weiyan Shi, Feifan Yan, Ryan Hou, Jingwen Zhang, Saurav Sahay, and Zhou Yu. 2022a. Seamlessly integrating factual information and social content with persuasive dialogue. In *Proceedings of the 2nd Conference of the Asia-Pacific Chapter of the Association for Computational Linguistics and the 12th International Joint Conference on Natural Language Processing, AACL/IJCNLP 2022*, pages 399–413.

Yun-Nung Chen, Asli Celikyilmaz, and Dilek Hakkani-Tür. 2017b. Deep learning for dialogue systems. In *Proceedings of the 55th Annual Meeting of the Association for Computational Linguistics: Tutorial Abstracts*, pages 8–14.

Zhi Chen, Lu Chen, Bei Chen, Libo Qin, Yuncong Liu, Su Zhu, Jian-Guang Lou, and Kai Yu. 2022b. Unidu: Towards A unified generative dialogue understanding framework. In *Proceedings of the 23rd Annual Meeting of the Special Interest Group on Discourse and Dialogue, SIGDIAL 2022*, pages 442–455.

Zhiyu Chen, Bing Liu, Seungwhan Moon, Chinnadhurai Sankar, Paul A. Crook, and William Yang Wang. 2022c. KETOD: knowledge-enriched task-oriented dialogue. In *Findings of the Association for Computational Linguistics: NAACL 2022*, pages 2581–2593.

Yi Cheng, Wenge Liu, Wenjie Li, Jiashuo Wang, Ruihui Zhao, Bang Liu, Xiaodan Liang, and Yefeng Zheng. 2022. Improving multi-turn emotional support dialogue generation with lookahead strategy planning. *CoRR*, abs/2210.04242.

Ssu Chiu, Maolin Li, Yen-Ting Lin, and Yun-Nung Chen. 2022. Salesbot: Transitioning from chit-chat to task-oriented dialogues. In *Proceedings of the 60th Annual Meeting of the Association for Computational Linguistics, ACL 2022*, pages 6143–6158.

Eunsol Choi, He He, Mohit Iyyer, Mark Yatskar, Wen-tau Yih, Yejin Choi, Percy Liang, and Luke Zettlemoyer. 2018. Quac: Question answering in context. In *Proceedings of the 2018 Conference on Empirical Methods in Natural Language Processing*, pages 2174–2184.

Jeffrey Dalton, Sophie Fischer, Paul Owoicho, Filip Radlinski, Federico Rossetto, Johanne R. Trippas, and Hamed Zamani. 2022. Conversational information seeking: Theory and application. In *SIGIR '22: The 45th International ACM SIGIR Conference on Research and Development in Information Retrieval*, pages 3455–3458.

Yang Deng, Wenqiang Lei, Wenxuan Zhang, Wai Lam, and Tat-Seng Chua. 2022a. PACIFIC: towards proactive conversational question answering over tabular and textual data in finance. *CoRR*, abs/2210.08817.

Yang Deng, Yaliang Li, Fei Sun, Bolin Ding, and Wai Lam. 2021. Unified conversational recommendation policy learning via graph-based reinforcement learning. In *SIGIR '21: The 44th International ACM SIGIR Conference on Research and Development in Information Retrieval*, pages 1431–1441.

Yang Deng, Wenxuan Zhang, Wai Lam, Hong Cheng, and Helen Meng. 2022b. User satisfaction estimation with sequential dialogue act modeling in goal-oriented conversational systems. In *WWW '22: The ACM Web Conference 2022*, pages 2998–3008.

Yang Deng, Wenxuan Zhang, Weiwen Xu, Wenqiang Lei, Tat-Seng Chua, and Wai Lam. 2022c. A unified multi-task learning framework for multi-goal conversational recommender systems. *CoRR*, abs/2204.06923.

Oxford English Dictionary. 1989. Oxford english dictionary. *Simpson, Ja & Weiner, Esc*, 3.

Ritam Dutt, Sayan Sinha, Rishabh Joshi, Surya Shekhar Chakraborty, Meredith Riggs, Xinru Yan, Haogang Bao, and Carolyn P. Rosé. 2021. Resper: Computationally modelling resisting strategies in persuasive conversations. In *Proceedings of the 16th Conference of the European Chapter of the Association for Computational Linguistics: Main Volume, EACL 2021*, pages 78–90.

Nouha Dziri, Sivan Milton, Mo Yu, Osmar R. Zaïane, and Siva Reddy. 2022. On the origin of hallucinations in conversational models: Is it the datasets or the models? In *Proceedings of the 2022 Conference of the North American Chapter of the Association for Computational Linguistics: Human Language Technologies, NAACL 2022*, pages 5271–5285.

Jianfeng Gao, Michel Galley, and Lihong Li. 2018. Neural approaches to conversational AI. In *Proceedings of ACL 2018, Tutorial Abstracts*, pages 2–7.

Jianfeng Gao, Michel Galley, and Lihong Li. 2019. Neural approaches to conversational AI. *Found. Trends Inf. Retr.*, 13(2-3):127–298.

Jianfeng Gao, Chenyan Xiong, and Paul Bennett. 2020. Recent advances in conversational information retrieval. In *Proceedings of the 43rd International ACM SIGIR conference on research and development in Information Retrieval, SIGIR 2020*, pages 2421–2424.

Jianfeng Gao, Chenyan Xiong, Paul Bennett, and Nick Craswell. 2022. Neural approaches to conversational information retrieval. *CoRR*, abs/2201.05176.

Adam M Grant and Susan J Ashford. 2008. The dynamics of proactivity at work. *Research in organizational behavior*, 28:3–34.

Meiqi Guo, Mingda Zhang, Siva Reddy, and Malihe Alikhani. 2021. Abg-coqa: Clarifying ambiguity in conversational question answering. In *AKBC 2021*.

Prakhar Gupta, Harsh Jhamtani, and Jeffrey P. Bigham. 2022. Target-guided dialogue response generation using commonsense and data augmentation. In *Findings of the Association for Computational Linguistics: NAACL 2022*, pages 1301–1317.

He He, Derek Chen, Anusha Balakrishnan, and Percy Liang. 2018. Decoupling strategy and generation in negotiation dialogues. In *Proceedings of the 2018 Conference on Empirical Methods in Natural Language Processing*, pages 2333–2343.

Or Honovich, Leshem Choshen, Roee Aharoni, Ella Neeman, Idan Szpektor, and Omri Abend. 2021. q^2: Evaluating factual consistency in knowledge-grounded dialogues via question generation and question answering. In *Proceedings of the 2021 Conference on Empirical Methods in Natural Language Processing, EMNLP 2021*, pages 7856–7870.

Zhiqiang Hu, Roy Ka-Wei Lee, and Nancy F. Chen. 2022. Are current task-oriented dialogue systems able to satisfy impolite users? *CoRR*, abs/2210.12942.

Minlie Huang, Xiaoyan Zhu, and Jianfeng Gao. 2020. Challenges in building intelligent open-domain dialog systems. *ACM Trans. Inf. Syst.*, 38(3):21:1–21:32.

Wenlong Huang, Pieter Abbeel, Deepak Pathak, and Igor Mordatch. 2022. Language models as zero-shot planners: Extracting actionable knowledge for embodied agents. In *International Conference on Machine Learning, ICML 2022*, volume 162, pages 9118–9147.

Rishabh Joshi, Vidhisha Balachandran, Shikhar Vashishth, Alan W. Black, and Yulia Tsvetkov. 2021. Dialograph: Incorporating interpretable strategy-graph networks into negotiation dialogues. In *9th International Conference on Learning Representations, ICLR 2021*.

Hyunwoo Kim, Youngjae Yu, Liwei Jiang, Ximing Lu, Daniel Khashabi, Gunhee Kim, Yejin Choi, and Maarten Sap. 2022. Prosocialdialog: A prosocial backbone for conversational agents. *CoRR*, abs/2205.12688.

Yosuke Kishinami, Reina Akama, Shiki Sato, Ryoko Tokuhisa, Jun Suzuki, and Kentaro Inui. 2022. Target-guided open-domain conversation planning. In *COLING 2022*, pages 660–668.

Wenqiang Lei, Xiangnan He, Yisong Miao, Qingyun Wu, Richang Hong, Min-Yen Kan, and Tat-Seng Chua. 2020a. Estimation-action-reflection: Towards deep interaction between conversational and recommender systems. In *WSDM 2020*, pages 304–312.

Wenqiang Lei, Xisen Jin, Min-Yen Kan, Zhaochun Ren, Xiangnan He, and Dawei Yin. 2018. Sequicity: Simplifying task-oriented dialogue systems with single sequence-to-sequence architectures. In *Proceedings of the 56th Annual Meeting of the Association for Computational Linguistics, ACL 2018*, pages 1437–1447.

Wenqiang Lei, Gangyi Zhang, Xiangnan He, Yisong Miao, Xiang Wang, Liang Chen, and Tat-Seng Chua. 2020b. Interactive path reasoning on graph for conversational recommendation. In *KDD '20: The 26th ACM SIGKDD Conference on Knowledge Discovery and Data Mining*, pages 2073–2083.

Wenqiang Lei, Yao Zhang, Feifan Song, Hongru Liang, Jiaxin Mao, Jiancheng Lv, Zhenglu Yang, and Tat-Seng Chua. 2022. Interacting with non-cooperative user: A new paradigm for proactive dialogue policy. In *SIGIR '22: The 45th International ACM SIGIR Conference on Research and Development in Information Retrieval*, pages 212–222.

Haoran Li, Yangqiu Song, and Lixin Fan. 2022a. You don't know my favorite color: Preventing dialogue representations from revealing speakers' private personas. In *Proceedings of the 2022 Conference of the North American Chapter of the Association for Computational Linguistics: Human Language Technologies, NAACL 2022*, pages 5858–5870.

Huihan Li, Tianyu Gao, Manan Goenka, and Danqi Chen. 2022b. Ditch the gold standard: Re-evaluating conversational question answering. In *Proceedings of the 60th Annual Meeting of the Association for Computational Linguistics, ACL 2022*, pages 8074–8085.

Raymond Li, Samira Ebrahimi Kahou, Hannes Schulz, Vincent Michalski, Laurent Charlin, and Chris Pal. 2018. Towards deep conversational recommendations. In *Advances in Neural Information Processing Systems 31: Annual Conference on Neural Information Processing Systems 2018, NeurIPS 2018*, pages 9748–9758.

Yanran Li, Hui Su, Xiaoyu Shen, Wenjie Li, Ziqiang Cao, and Shuzi Niu. 2017. Dailydialog: A manually labelled multi-turn dialogue dataset. In *Proceedings of the Eighth International Joint Conference on Natural Language Processing, IJCNLP 2017*, pages 986–995.

Yu Li, Kun Qian, Weiyan Shi, and Zhou Yu. 2020. End-to-end trainable non-collaborative dialog system. In *The Thirty-Fourth AAAI Conference on Artificial Intelligence, AAAI 2020*, pages 8293–8302.

Jiawei Liu, Kaisong Song, Yangyang Kang, Guoxiu He, Zhuoren Jiang, Changlong Sun, Wei Lu, and Xiaozhong Liu. 2021a. A role-selected sharing network for joint machine-human chatting handoff and service satisfaction analysis. In *Proceedings of the 2021 Conference on Empirical Methods in Natural Language Processing, EMNLP 2021*, pages 9731–9741.

Siyang Liu, Chujie Zheng, Orianna Demasi, Sahand Sabour, Yu Li, Zhou Yu, Yong Jiang, and Minlie Huang. 2021b. Towards emotional support dialog systems. In *Proceedings of the 59th Annual Meeting of the Association for Computational Linguistics and the 11th International Joint Conference on Natural Language Processing, ACL/IJCNLP 2021*, pages 3469–3483.

Zeming Liu, Haifeng Wang, Zheng-Yu Niu, Hua Wu, Wanxiang Che, and Ting Liu. 2020. Towards conversational recommendation over multi-type dialogs. In *Proceedings of the 58th Annual Meeting of the Association for Computational Linguistics, ACL 2020*, pages 1036–1049.

Zeming Liu, Jun Xu, Zeyang Lei, Haifeng Wang, Zheng-Yu Niu, and Hua Wu. 2022. Where to go for the holidays: Towards mixed-type dialogs for clarification of user goals. In *Proceedings of the 60th Annual Meeting of the Association for Computational Linguistics, ACL 2022*, pages 1024–1034.

Kshitij Mishra, Azlaan Mustafa Samad, Palak Totala, and Asif Ekbal. 2022. PEPDS: A polite and empathetic persuasive dialogue system for charity donation. In *Proceedings of the 29th International Conference on Computational Linguistics, COLING 2022*, pages 424–440.

Jinjie Ni, Vlad Pandelea, Tom Young, Haicang Zhou, and Erik Cambria. 2022. Hitkg: Towards goal-oriented conversations via multi-hierarchy learning. In *Thirty-Sixth AAAI Conference on Artificial Intelligence, AAAI 2022*, pages 11112–11120.

Baolin Peng, Chunyuan Li, Zhu Zhang, Chenguang Zhu, Jinchao Li, and Jianfeng Gao. 2021. RADDLE: an evaluation benchmark and analysis platform for robust task-oriented dialog systems. In *Proceedings of the 59th Annual Meeting of the Association for*

Computational Linguistics and the 11th International Joint Conference on Natural Language Processing, ACL/IJCNLP 2021, pages 4418–4429.

Jinghui Qin, Zheng Ye, Jianheng Tang, and Xiaodan Liang. 2020. Dynamic knowledge routing network for target-guided open-domain conversation. In *AAAI 2020*, pages 8657–8664.

Minghui Qiu, Xinjing Huang, Cen Chen, Feng Ji, Chen Qu, Wei Wei, Jun Huang, and Yin Zhang. 2021. Reinforced history backtracking for conversational question answering. In *Thirty-Fifth AAAI Conference on Artificial Intelligence, AAAI 2021*, pages 13718–13726.

Konigari Rachna, Saurabh Ramola, Vijay Vardhan Alluri, and Manish Shrivastava. 2021. Topic shift detection for mixed initiative response. In *SIGdial 20211*, pages 161–166.

Siva Reddy, Danqi Chen, and Christopher D. Manning. 2019. Coqa: A conversational question answering challenge. *Trans. Assoc. Comput. Linguistics*, 7:249–266.

Stephen Roller, Emily Dinan, Naman Goyal, Da Ju, Mary Williamson, Yinhan Liu, Jing Xu, Myle Ott, Eric Michael Smith, Y-Lan Boureau, and Jason Weston. 2021. Recipes for building an open-domain chatbot. In *Proceedings of the 16th Conference of the European Chapter of the Association for Computational Linguistics: Main Volume, EACL 2021,*, pages 300–325.

Martin Saveski, Brandon Roy, and Deb Roy. 2021. The structure of toxic conversations on twitter. In *WWW '21: The Web Conference 2021*, pages 1086–1097.

J Schulman, B Zoph, C Kim, J Hilton, J Menick, J Weng, JFC Uribe, L Fedus, L Metz, M Pokorny, et al. 2022. Chatgpt: Optimizing language models for dialogue.

John R Searle. 1992. *The rediscovery of the mind*. MIT press.

Ivan Sekulic, Mohammad Aliannejadi, and Fabio Crestani. 2022. Evaluating mixed-initiative conversational search systems via user simulation. In *WSDM '22: The Fifteenth ACM International Conference on Web Search and Data Mining*, pages 888–896.

Weiyan Shi, Aiqi Cui, Evan Li, Ruoxi Jia, and Zhou Yu. 2022. Selective differential privacy for language modeling. In *Proceedings of the 2022 Conference of the North American Chapter of the Association for Computational Linguistics: Human Language Technologies, NAACL 2022*, pages 2848–2859.

Weiyan Shi, Yu Li, Saurav Sahay, and Zhou Yu. 2021. Refine and imitate: Reducing repetition and inconsistency in persuasion dialogues via reinforcement learning and human demonstration. In *Findings of the Association for Computational Linguistics: EMNLP 2021*, pages 3478–3492.

Kurt Shuster, Jing Xu, Mojtaba Komeili, Da Ju, Eric Michael Smith, Stephen Roller, Megan Ung, Moya Chen, Kushal Arora, Joshua Lane, Morteza Behrooz, William Ngan, Spencer Poff, Naman Goyal, Arthur Szlam, Y-Lan Boureau, Melanie Kambadur, and Jason Weston. 2022. Blenderbot 3: a deployed conversational agent that continually learns to responsibly engage. *CoRR*, abs/2208.03188.

Pei-Hao Su, Nikola Mrkšić, Iñigo Casanueva, and Ivan Vulić. 2018. Deep learning for conversational AI. In *Proceedings of the 2018 Conference of the North American Chapter of the Association for Computational Linguistics: Tutorial Abstracts*, pages 27–32.

Yixuan Su, Lei Shu, Elman Mansimov, Arshit Gupta, Deng Cai, Yi-An Lai, and Yi Zhang. 2022. Multi-task pre-training for plug-and-play task-oriented dialogue system. In *Proceedings of the 60th Annual Meeting of the Association for Computational Linguistics, ACL 2022*, pages 4661–4676.

Hao Sun, Guangxuan Xu, Jiawen Deng, Jiale Cheng, Chujie Zheng, Hao Zhou, Nanyun Peng, Xiaoyan Zhu, and Minlie Huang. 2022. On the safety of conversational models: Taxonomy, dataset, and benchmark. In *Findings of the Association for Computational Linguistics: ACL 2022*, pages 3906–3923.

Kai Sun, Seungwhan Moon, Paul A. Crook, Stephen Roller, Becka Silvert, Bing Liu, Zhiguang Wang, Honglei Liu, Eunjoon Cho, and Claire Cardie. 2021. Adding chit-chat to enhance task-oriented dialogues. In *Proceedings of the 2021 Conference of the North American Chapter of the Association for Computational Linguistics: Human Language Technologies, NAACL-HLT 2021*, pages 1570–1583.

Jianheng Tang, Tiancheng Zhao, Chenyan Xiong, Xiaodan Liang, Eric P. Xing, and Zhiting Hu. 2019. Target-guided open-domain conversation. In *ACL 2019*, pages 5624–5634.

Romal Thoppilan, Daniel De Freitas, Jamie Hall, Noam Shazeer, Apoorv Kulshreshtha, Heng-Tze Cheng, Alicia Jin, Taylor Bos, Leslie Baker, Yu Du, YaGuang Li, Hongrae Lee, Huaixiu Steven Zheng, Amin Ghafouri, Marcelo Menegali, Yanping Huang, Maxim Krikun, Dmitry Lepikhin, James Qin, Dehao Chen, Yuanzhong Xu, Zhifeng Chen, Adam Roberts, Maarten Bosma, Yanqi Zhou, Chung-Ching Chang, Igor Krivokon, Will Rusch, Marc Pickett, Kathleen S. Meier-Hellstern, Meredith Ringel Morris, Tulsee Doshi, Renelito Delos Santos, Toju Duke, Johnny Soraker, Ben Zevenbergen, Vinodkumar Prabhakaran, Mark Diaz, Ben Hutchinson, Kristen Olson, Alejandra Molina, Erin Hoffman-John, Josh Lee, Lora Aroyo, Ravi Rajakumar, Alena Butryna, Matthew Lamm, Viktoriya Kuzmina, Joe Fenton, Aaron Cohen, Rachel Bernstein, Ray Kurzweil, Blaise Aguera-Arcas, Claire Cui, Marian Croak, Ed H. Chi, and Quoc Le. 2022. Lamda: Language models for dialog applications. *CoRR*, abs/2201.08239.

Quan Tu, Yanran Li, Jianwei Cui, Bin Wang, Ji-Rong Wen, and Rui Yan. 2022. MISC: A mixed strategy-aware model integrating COMET for emotional support conversation. In *Proceedings of the 60th Annual Meeting of the Association for Computational Linguistics, ACL 2022*, pages 308–319.

Megan Ung, Jing Xu, and Y-Lan Boureau. 2022. Saferdialogues: Taking feedback gracefully after conversational safety failures. In *Proceedings of the 60th Annual Meeting of the Association for Computational Linguistics, ACL 2022*, pages 6462–6481.

Lingzhi Wang, Shafiq R. Joty, Wei Gao, Xingshan Zeng, and Kam-Fai Wong. 2022. Improving conversational recommender system via contextual and time-aware modeling with less domain-specific knowledge. *CoRR*, abs/2209.11386.

Xuewei Wang, Weiyan Shi, Richard Kim, Yoojung Oh, Sijia Yang, Jingwen Zhang, and Zhou Yu. 2019. Persuasion for good: Towards a personalized persuasive dialogue system for social good. In *Proceedings of the 57th Conference of the Association for Computational Linguistics, ACL 2019*, pages 5635–5649.

Qingyang Wu, Yichi Zhang, Yu Li, and Zhou Yu. 2021. Alternating recurrent dialog model with large-scale pre-trained language models. In *Proceedings of the 16th Conference of the European Chapter of the Association for Computational Linguistics: Main Volume, EACL 2021*, pages 1292–1301.

Wenquan Wu, Zhen Guo, Xiangyang Zhou, Hua Wu, Xiyuan Zhang, Rongzhong Lian, and Haifeng Wang. 2019. Proactive human-machine conversation with explicit conversation goal. In *ACL 2019*, pages 3794–3804.

Huiyuan Xie, Zhenghao Liu, Chenyan Xiong, Zhiyuan Liu, and Ann A. Copestake. 2021. TIAGE: A benchmark for topic-shift aware dialog modeling. In *Findings of ACL: EMNLP 2021*, pages 1684–1690.

Jun Xu, Haifeng Wang, Zhengyu Niu, Hua Wu, and Wanxiang Che. 2020. Knowledge graph grounded goal planning for open-domain conversation generation. In *The Thirty-Fourth AAAI Conference on Artificial Intelligence, AAAI 2020*, pages 9338–9345.

Atsuki Yamaguchi, Kosui Iwasa, and Katsuhide Fujita. 2021. Dialogue act-based breakdown detection in negotiation dialogues. In *Proceedings of the 16th Conference of the European Chapter of the Association for Computational Linguistics: Main Volume, EACL 2021*, pages 745–757.

Rui Yan, Juntao Li, and Zhou Yu. 2022. Deep learning for dialogue systems: Chit-chat and beyond. *Foundations and Trends in Information Retrieval*, 15(5):417–589.

Runzhe Yang, Jingxiao Chen, and Karthik Narasimhan. 2021. Improving dialog systems for negotiation with personality modeling. In *Proceedings of the 59th Annual Meeting of the Association for Computational Linguistics and the 11th International Joint Conference on Natural Language Processing, ACL/IJCNLP 2021*, pages 681–693.

Wei Yang, Luchen Tan, Chunwei Lu, Anqi Cui, Han Li, Xi Chen, Kun Xiong, Muzi Wang, Ming Li, Jian Pei, and Jimmy Lin. 2019. Detecting customer complaint escalation with recurrent neural networks and manually-engineered features. In *Proceedings of the 2019 Conference of the North American Chapter of the Association for Computational Linguistics: Human Language Technologies, NAACL-HLT 2019*, pages 56–63.

Zhitong Yang, Bo Wang, Jinfeng Zhou, Yue Tan, Dongming Zhao, Kun Huang, Ruifang He, and Yuexian Hou. 2022. Topkg: Target-oriented dialog via global planning on knowledge graph. In *Proceedings of the 29th International Conference on Computational Linguistics, COLING 2022*, pages 745–755.

Shunyu Yao, Jeffrey Zhao, Dian Yu, Nan Du, Izhak Shafran, Karthik Narasimhan, and Yuan Cao. 2022. React: Synergizing reasoning and acting in language models. *CoRR*, abs/2210.03629.

Tom Young, Frank Xing, Vlad Pandelea, Jinjie Ni, and Erik Cambria. 2022. Fusing task-oriented and open-domain dialogues in conversational agents. In *Thirty-Sixth AAAI Conference on Artificial Intelligence, AAAI 2022*, pages 11622–11629.

Hamed Zamani, Susan T. Dumais, Nick Craswell, Paul N. Bennett, and Gord Lueck. 2020. Generating clarifying questions for information retrieval. In *WWW 2020*, pages 418–428.

Hamed Zamani, Johanne R. Trippas, Jeff Dalton, and Filip Radlinski. 2022. Conversational information seeking. *CoRR*, abs/2201.08808.

Chen Zhang, Yiming Chen, Luis Fernando D'Haro, Yan Zhang, Thomas Friedrichs, Grandee Lee, and Haizhou Li. 2021a. Dynaeval: Unifying turn and dialogue level evaluation. In *Proceedings of the 59th Annual Meeting of the Association for Computational Linguistics and the 11th International Joint Conference on Natural Language Processing, ACL/IJCNLP 2021*, pages 5676–5689.

Jun Zhang, Yan Yang, Chencai Chen, Liang He, and Zhou Yu. 2021b. KERS: A knowledge-enhanced framework for recommendation dialog systems with multiple subgoals. In *Findings of the Association for Computational Linguistics: EMNLP 2021*, pages 1092–1101.

Saizheng Zhang, Emily Dinan, Jack Urbanek, Arthur Szlam, Douwe Kiela, and Jason Weston. 2018a. Personalizing dialogue agents: I have a dog, do you have pets too? In *Proceedings of the 56th Annual Meeting of the Association for Computational Linguistics, ACL 2018*, pages 2204–2213.

Shuo Zhang and Krisztian Balog. 2020. Evaluating conversational recommender systems via user simulation. In *KDD '20: The 26th ACM SIGKDD Conference on Knowledge Discovery and Data Mining*, pages 1512–1520.

Yongfeng Zhang, Xu Chen, Qingyao Ai, Liu Yang, and W. Bruce Croft. 2018b. Towards conversational search and recommendation: System ask, user respond. In *CIKM 2018*, pages 177–186.

Xinyan Zhao, Bin He, Yasheng Wang, Yitong Li, Fei Mi, Yajiao Liu, Xin Jiang, Qun Liu, and Huanhuan Chen. 2022. Unids: A unified dialogue system for chit-chat and task-oriented dialogues. In *Proceedings of the Second DialDoc Workshop on Document-grounded Dialogue and Conversational Question Answering, DialDoc@ACL 2022*, pages 13–22.

Peixiang Zhong, Yong Liu, Hao Wang, and Chunyan Miao. 2021. Keyword-guided neural conversational model. In *Thirty-Fifth AAAI Conference on Artificial Intelligence, AAAI 2021*, pages 14568–14576.

Yiheng Zhou, Yulia Tsvetkov, Alan W. Black, and Zhou Yu. 2020. Augmenting non-collaborative dialog systems with explicit semantic and strategic dialog history. In *8th International Conference on Learning Representations, ICLR 2020*.

Caleb Ziems, Jane A. Yu, Yi-Chia Wang, Alon Y. Halevy, and Diyi Yang. 2022. The moral integrity corpus: A benchmark for ethical dialogue systems. In *Proceedings of the 60th Annual Meeting of the Association for Computational Linguistics, ACL 2022*, pages 3755–3773.

Cutting-Edge Tutorial: Complex Reasoning over Natural Language

Wenting Zhao
Cornell University
wzhao@cs.cornell.edu

Mor Geva*
Google Research
pipek@google.com

Bill Yuchen Lin*
Allen Institute for AI
yuchenl@allenai.org

Michihiro Yasunaga*
Stanford University
myasu@cs.stanford.edu

Aman Madaan*
Carnegie Mellon University
amadaan@cs.cmu.edu

Tao Yu*
The University of Hong Kong
tyu@cs.hku.hk

1 Tutorial Overview

Teaching machines to reason over texts has been a long-standing goal of natural language processing (NLP). To this end, researchers have designed a diverse set of complex reasoning tasks that involve compositional reasoning (Geva et al., 2021; Trivedi et al., 2022), knowledge retrieval (Yang et al., 2018; Kwiatkowski et al., 2019), grounding (Budzianowski et al., 2018; Xie et al., 2022; Shi et al., 2021), commonsense reasoning (Talmor et al., 2021a; Lin et al., 2020), etc.

A standard choice for building systems that perform a desired type of reasoning is to fine-tune a pretrained language model (LM) on specific downstream tasks. However, recent research has demonstrated that such a straightforward approach is often brittle. For example, Elazar et al. (2021) and Branco et al. (2021) show that, on question-answering (QA) tasks, similar performance can be achieved with questions removed from the inputs. Min et al. (2019), Chen and Durrett (2019), and Tang et al. (2021) show that models trained on multi-hop QA do not generalize to answer single-hop questions. The reasoning capabilities of these models thus remain at a surface level, i.e., exploiting data patterns. Consequently, augmenting LMs with techniques that make them robust and effective becomes an active research area.

We will start the tutorial by providing an overview of complex reasoning tasks where the standard application of pretrained language models fails (in Sec 2). This tutorial then reviews recent promising directions for tackling these tasks (in Sec 3). Specifically, we focus on the following groups of approaches that explicitly consider problem structures: (1) knowledge-augmented methods, where the knowledge is either incorporated during fine-tuning or pretraining; (2) few-shot prompting methods, which effectively guide the models to follow instructions; (3) neuro-symbolic methods, which produce explicit intermediate representations; and, (4) rationale-based methods, one of the most popular forms of the neuro-symbolic methods, which highlight subsets of input as explanations for individual model predictions. The tutorial materials are online at https://wenting-zhao.github.io/complex-reasoning-tutorial.

2 Problem Introduction

We will start with NLP tasks that require reasoning over multiple pieces of information in a provided context, covering various reasoning skills such as fact composition, mathematical reasoning, inferring semantic structures, and reasoning about entities (Yang et al., 2018; Yu et al., 2018; Budzianowski et al., 2018; Dua et al., 2019; Ho et al., 2020; Dasigi et al., 2019; Cobbe et al., 2021; Trivedi et al., 2022). Then, we will discuss benchmarks that combine multiple sources of information (i.e., modalities), e.g., paragraphs, tables, and images (Chen et al., 2020b; Talmor et al., 2021b; Pasupat and Liang, 2015; Chen et al., 2020a).

We will present open-domain setups where external knowledge should be integrated into the reasoning process (Geva et al., 2021; Onoe et al., 2021; Ferguson et al., 2020; Talmor and Berant, 2018). In addition, we will review tasks that require commonsense reasoning (Talmor et al., 2021a; Rudinger et al., 2020; Sap et al., 2019; Saha et al., 2021).

We will conclude this part by highlighting key practices for dataset creation, that increase data diversity and minimize annotation biases and reasoning shortcuts (Bartolo et al., 2020; Khot et al., 2020; Geva et al., 2019; Parmar et al., 2022).

3 Approaches

(1a) Knowledge-Augmented Fine-Tuning Tackling complex reasoning problems that require commonsense knowledge and entity-centric facts can

*Equal Contribution.

Proceedings of the 61st Annual Meeting of the Association for Computational Linguistics
Volume 6: Tutorial Abstracts, pages 11–20

benefit from access to external knowledge sources. How to incorporate knowledge during fine-tuning has thus been extensively studied. A general method is to retrieving knowledge facts relevant to given situations (e.g., questions) and fusing them with an LM-based neural module. External knowledge can be categorized into three forms: structured (e.g., knowledge graphs like ConceptNet (Speer et al., 2017)), unstructured (e.g., knowledge corpora such as Wikipedia and GenericsKB (Bhakthavatsalam et al., 2020)), and instance-based (i.e., annotated examples).

In this section, we will cover methods for these three forms of knowledge in a variety of reasoning problems. For structured knowledge, KagNet (Lin et al., 2019) is a typical method that focuses on fusing retrieved subgraphs from ConceptNet for fine-tuning LMs to perform commonsense reasoning. Follow-up works include MHGRN (Feng et al., 2020), QA-GNN (Yasunaga et al., 2021), and GreaseLM (Zhang et al., 2022b). For unstructured knowledge, we will introduce methods that encode a large knowledge corpus as neural memory modules to support knowledge retrieval for reasoning. We will start with DPR (Karpukhin et al., 2020), one of the most popular methods that embed Wikipedia as a dense matrix of fact embeddings. Then, we will cover DrKIT (Dhingra et al., 2020), which improves multi-hop reasoning ability by encoding sparse entity mentions. Additionally, we introduce DrFact (Lin et al., 2021), a fact-level extension for DrKIT that focuses on commonsense reasoning. For instance-based knowledge, a promising direction, we will also introduce methods such as RACo (Yu et al., 2022b), ReCross (Lin et al., 2022), and QEDB (Chen et al., 2022b), which aim to exploit annotated examples to enhance reasoning.

(1b) Knowledge-Augmented Pretraining. Pretraining performs self-supervised learning of representations from large-scale data, which holds the potential to help a broader range of downstream tasks. We will review recent efforts to incorporate knowledge and reasoning abilities into LMs during pretraining. We first discuss retrieval-augmented pretraining (Guu et al., 2020; Lewis et al., 2020a; Borgeaud et al., 2021; Yasunaga et al., 2022b), which retrieves relevant documents from an external memory and feeds them to the model as an additional input. This helps not only knowledge-intensive tasks but also some reasoning-intensive tasks because the models learn to process multiple documents for multi-hop reasoning (Yasunaga et al., 2022b). We then discuss works that integrate structured knowledge bases/graphs. For example, some use knowledge graphs to make additional pretraining objectives for LMs (Xiong et al., 2020; Shen et al., 2020; Wang et al., 2021; Liu et al., 2021; Yu et al., 2022a; Ke et al., 2021); others retrieve and feed entity or knowledge graph information as a direct input to the model (Zhang et al., 2019; Rosset et al., 2020; Liu et al., 2020; Sun et al., 2021; Agarwal et al., 2021; Sun et al., 2020; He et al., 2020; Yasunaga et al., 2022a). Recent works show that these retrieved knowledge graphs can provide LMs with scaffolds for performing complex reasoning over entities, such as logical and multi-hop reasoning (Yasunaga et al., 2022a).

(2) Few-Shot Prompting Approaches. The rise of large pretrained LMs, such as GPT-3 (Brown et al., 2020), OPT (Zhang et al., 2022a), and PaLM (Chowdhery et al., 2022), has unlocked the potential of few-shot prompting methods for a wide range of reasoning tasks. However, despite their strengths, these LMs in the few-shot prompting mode have peculiar failure modes, especially when it comes to complex reasoning tasks (Marcus, 2022). Further, the *prompt* has to be designed carefully, and it has been shown that seemingly innocuous changes to the prompt (e.g., order of examples or the format of text) can drastically impact the performance (Le Scao and Rush, 2021; Mishra et al., 2021). In response, several techniques have been developed to make few-shot prompting methods to be less susceptible to the exact prompt choice. This section will cover both a high-level overview of few-shot prompting and introduce specific classes of techniques that can further improve the few-shot prompting methods on complex reasoning tasks.

First, we will introduce prompt-design techniques like chain-of-thought prompting (Wei et al., 2022b) and least-to-most prompting (Wei et al., 2022c), which encourage an LM to generate reasoning steps as part of the solution, helping with problem decomposition and enhanced reasoning. Next, we will cover techniques that change the prompt dynamically for each input query. The methods covered in this part include selecting the training examples in the prompt (Liu et al., 2022a) and editing the prompt to incorporate feedback received on a similar-input (Madaan et al., 2022a).

Finally, we will cover techniques that leverage code-generation models for complex reasoning tasks. Representative techniques in this part will cover i) the use of code-generation model for structured commonsense reasoning (Madaan et al., 2022b), ii) algorithmic reasoning by expanding detailed instructions in the prompt (Zhou et al., 2022), and iii) generating chain-of-thought styled reasoning chains in Python code to tackle complex symbolic reasoning tasks (Gao et al., 2022).

(3) Neuro-Symbolic Approaches. Although performance on NLP tasks is dominated by neural *end-to-end* systems that directly map inputs to outputs (Devlin et al., 2019; Raffel et al., 2020), these approaches lack interpretability and robustness. *Symbolic* approaches, on the other hand, produce explicit intermediate reasoning trajectories such as logical forms, reasoning paths, or program code, which might then be executed to derive a final output (Zettlemoyer and Collins, 2005; Chen et al., 2019b, *i.a.*). Compared to both end-to-end and chain-of-thought methods (Wei et al., 2022a, *i.a.*), the reasoning processes produced by the symbolic methods are interpretable, and the resulting execution makes them more robust to input changes.

Researchers (Andreas et al., 2016; Liang et al., 2017; Gupta et al., 2019; Khot et al., 2021; Zhu et al., 2022; Cheng et al., 2022; Gao et al., 2022; Schick et al., 2023, *i.a.*) also propose to combine neural modules and symbolic components to leverage advantages of both approaches. More specifically, Neural-Symbolic Machines (Liang et al., 2017) adopt a seq-to-seq model to generate programs and a Lisp interpreter that performs program execution. (Chen et al., 2019b) designs a domain-specific language for question answering over text. BREAK (Wolfson et al., 2020) proposes a meaningful representation, QDMR, that decomposes the question into multiple steps. Thorne et al. (2021) propose a mixed pipeline of logic forms and neural networks, aiming at solving the scale problem and noisy, messy data over a natural language database.

Another stream of works called neural module networks (Andreas et al., 2016; Das et al., 2018; Gupta et al., 2019) propose to generate symbolic programs that are further softly executed by the corresponding neural modules. Khot et al. (2021) propose text module networks to solve complex tasks by decomposing them into simpler ones solvable by existing QA models and a symbolic calculator. However, most prior neural-symbolic methods require the elaborate human design of the symbolic language and the calibration of corresponding neural modules to tackle problems in a specific domain with large training data. Recently, Cheng et al. (2022) propose Binder, a new neural-symbolic system based on GPT-3 Codex (Chen et al., 2021) that supports *flexible* neural module calls that will enable *higher coverage* for the symbolic language, while only requiring *few annotations*. Also, Gao et al. (2022) introduce PAL, a new method based on Codex that generates executable programs as the intermediate reasoning steps and leverages a Python interpreter to derive final answers.

This section will begin by discussing the high-level comparison among the end-to-end, chain-of-thought, symbolic (e.g., semantic parsing), and neural-symbolic approaches. We will then move to provide a high-level overview of different neural-symbolic approaches. In this part, we will mainly focus on neural-symbolic approaches with LMs. Finally, we will cover recent techniques incorporating GPT-3 Codex in neural-symbolic approaches.

(4) Rationale-Based Approaches. Rationale-based approaches extract parts of input to be *reasoning certificates*, offering end users a way to evaluate the trustworthiness of the predictions. Based on reasoning types, rationales of different granularity are identified – they can be tokens, sentences, or documents (DeYoung et al., 2020; Kwiatkowski et al., 2019). NLP systems can benefit from rationales in several ways. Yang et al. (2018) show that providing rationales as additional supervision improves models' capacity to perform multi-hop reasoning. More recently, Chen et al. (2022a) demonstrate the potential of using such methods to build more robust NLP systems.

Existing methods for extracting rationales often require supervision; they either apply multi-task loss functions (Joshi et al., 2020; Groeneveld et al., 2020), or design specialized network architectures to incorporate inductive biases (Tu et al., 2019; Fang et al., 2020). Because rationale annotations are expensive to collect and not always available, recent effort has been devoted to semi-supervised and unsupervised methods. Chen et al. (2019a) leverage entity taggers to build silver reasoning chains used for rationale supervision. Glockner et al. (2020) and Atanasova et al. (2022) design unsupervised objectives for extracting rationales in multi-hop QA systems. Finally, latent-variable approaches are a natural fit for unsupervised learning (Lei et al., 2016; Zhou et al., 2020; Lewis et al.,

2020b). By modeling rationales as a latent variable, it provides a principled way to explicitly impose constraints in the reasoning process.

3.1 Schedule

1. Introduction & Motivations (15 min.)
2. Benchmarks & Evaluation (25 min.)
3. Knowledge-augmented Fine-tuning (25 min.)
4. Knowledge-augmented Pretraining (25 min.)
5. Break (30 minutes)
6. Neuro-Symbolic Approaches (25 min.)
7. Few-shot Prompting Approaches (25 min.)
8. Rationale-Based Approaches (25 min.)
9. Concluding discussion (15 min.)

4 Instructor information

Wenting Zhao is a Ph.D. student in Computer Science at Cornell University. Her research focuses on the intersection of reasoning and NLP. She is especially interested in developing explainable methods for complex reasoning problems.

Mor Geva is a postdoctoral researcher, now at Google Research and previously at the Allen Institute for AI. Her research focuses on debugging the inner workings of black-box NLP models, to increase their transparency, control their operation, and improve their reasoning abilities. She is organizing the next edition of the Workshop on Commonsense Reasoning and Representation.

Bill Yuchen Lin is a postdoctoral researcher at the Allen Institute for AI. He obtained his Ph.D. at USC advised by Prof. Xiang Ren. His research goal is to teach machines to think, talk, and act with commonsense knowledge and commonsense reasoning ability as humans do. He was a co-author of the tutorial on *Knowledge-Augmented Methods for Natural Language Processing* and the *Workshop on Commonsense Representation and Reasoning* at ACL 2022.

Michihiro Yasunaga is a Ph.D. student in Computer Science at Stanford University. His research interest is in developing generalizable models with knowledge, including commonsense, science, and reasoning abilities. He co-organized the Workshop on Structured and Unstructured Knowledge Integration (SUKI) at NAACL 2022.

Aman Madaan is a Ph.D. student at the School of Computer Science, Carnegie Mellon University. He is interested in large language models, feedback-driven generation, and the intersection of code generation and natural language reasoning. He helped organize the 1st and 2nd Workshops on Natural Language Generation, Evaluation, and Metrics (GEM) at ACL 2021 and EMNLP 2022.

Tao Yu is an assistant professor of computer science at The University of Hong Kong. He completed his Ph.D. at Yale University and was a postdoctoral fellow at the University of Washington. He works on executable language understanding, such as semantic parsing and code generation, and large LMs. Tao is the recipient of an Amazon Research Award. He co-organized multiple workshops in Semantic Parsing and Structured and Unstructured Knowledge Integration at EMNLP and NAACL.

5 Other Information

Reading List Rogers et al. (2022); Storks et al. (2019); Liu et al. (2022b); Lyu et al. (2022); Wiegreffe and Marasović (2021); Andreas et al. (2016); Cheng et al. (2022); Gao et al. (2022).

Breadth We estimate that approximately 30% of the tutorial will center around work done by the presenters. This tutorial categorizes promising approaches for complex reasoning tasks into several groups, and each of this group includes a significant amount of other researchers' works.

Diversity considerations The challenges of building robust and generalizable NLP systems exist in every language. The methods covered in this tutorial are language-agnostic and can be extended to non-English context.

For instructors, they all have different affiliations (i.e., Cornell, Google, Stanford, USC, HKU, and CMU). They are three PhD students, two postdoctoral researchers, and one assistant professor; two of the instructors are female.

Prerequisites Following knowledge is assumed:

- Machine Learning: basic probability theory, supervised learning, transformer models
- NLP: Familiarity with pretrained LMs; standard NLP tasks such as question answering, text generation, etc.

Estimated number of participants 150.

Preferable venue ACL.

Targeted audience Researchers and practitioners who seek to develop a background in complex reasoning tasks where standard application of pretrained language models fail. By providing a systematic overview of recent promising approaches for these tasks, this tutorial hopefully reveals new research opportunities to the audience.

References

Oshin Agarwal, Heming Ge, Siamak Shakeri, and Rami Al-Rfou. 2021. Knowledge graph based synthetic corpus generation for knowledge-enhanced language model pre-training. In *North American Chapter of the Association for Computational Linguistics (NAACL)*.

Jacob Andreas, Marcus Rohrbach, Trevor Darrell, and Dan Klein. 2016. Neural module networks. In *Proceedings of the IEEE conference on computer vision and pattern recognition*, pages 39–48.

Pepa Atanasova, Jakob Grue Simonsen, Christina Lioma, and Isabelle Augenstein. 2022. Diagnostics-guided explanation generation. In *Proceedings of the AAAI Conference on Artificial Intelligence*, volume 36, pages 10445–10453.

Max Bartolo, Alastair Roberts, Johannes Welbl, Sebastian Riedel, and Pontus Stenetorp. 2020. Beat the AI: Investigating adversarial human annotation for reading comprehension. *Transactions of the Association for Computational Linguistics*, 8:662–678.

Sumithra Bhakthavatsalam, Chloe Anastasiades, and Peter Clark. 2020. Genericskb: A knowledge base of generic statements. *ArXiv*, abs/2005.00660.

Sebastian Borgeaud, Arthur Mensch, Jordan Hoffmann, Trevor Cai, Eliza Rutherford, Katie Millican, George van den Driessche, Jean-Baptiste Lespiau, Bogdan Damoc, Aidan Clark, et al. 2021. Improving language models by retrieving from trillions of tokens. *arXiv preprint arXiv:2112.04426*.

Ruben Branco, António Branco, João António Rodrigues, and João Ricardo Silva. 2021. Shortcutted commonsense: Data spuriousness in deep learning of commonsense reasoning. In *Proceedings of the 2021 Conference on Empirical Methods in Natural Language Processing*, pages 1504–1521, Online and Punta Cana, Dominican Republic. Association for Computational Linguistics.

Tom Brown, Benjamin Mann, Nick Ryder, Melanie Subbiah, Jared D Kaplan, Prafulla Dhariwal, Arvind Neelakantan, Pranav Shyam, Girish Sastry, Amanda Askell, et al. 2020. Language models are few-shot learners. *Advances in neural information processing systems*, 33:1877–1901.

Paweł Budzianowski, Tsung-Hsien Wen, Bo-Hsiang Tseng, Iñigo Casanueva, Stefan Ultes, Osman Ramadan, and Milica Gašić. 2018. MultiWOZ - a large-scale multi-domain Wizard-of-Oz dataset for task-oriented dialogue modelling. In *Proceedings of the 2018 Conference on Empirical Methods in Natural Language Processing*, pages 5016–5026, Brussels, Belgium. Association for Computational Linguistics.

Howard Chen, Jacqueline He, Karthik Narasimhan, and Danqi Chen. 2022a. Can rationalization improve robustness? In *Proceedings of the 2022 Conference of the North American Chapter of the Association for Computational Linguistics: Human Language Technologies*, pages 3792–3805, Seattle, United States. Association for Computational Linguistics.

Jifan Chen and Greg Durrett. 2019. Understanding dataset design choices for multi-hop reasoning. In *Proceedings of the 2019 Conference of the North American Chapter of the Association for Computational Linguistics: Human Language Technologies, Volume 1 (Long and Short Papers)*, pages 4026–4032, Minneapolis, Minnesota. Association for Computational Linguistics.

Jifan Chen, Shih-ting Lin, and Greg Durrett. 2019a. Multi-hop question answering via reasoning chains. *arXiv preprint arXiv:1910.02610*.

Mark Chen, Jerry Tworek, Heewoo Jun, Qiming Yuan, Henrique Ponde de Oliveira Pinto, Jared Kaplan, Harri Edwards, Yuri Burda, Nicholas Joseph, Greg Brockman, Alex Ray, Raul Puri, Gretchen Krueger, Michael Petrov, Heidy Khlaaf, Girish Sastry, Pamela Mishkin, Brooke Chan, Scott Gray, Nick Ryder, Mikhail Pavlov, Alethea Power, Lukasz Kaiser, Mohammad Bavarian, Clemens Winter, Philippe Tillet, Felipe Petroski Such, Dave Cummings, Matthias Plappert, Fotios Chantzis, Elizabeth Barnes, Ariel Herbert-Voss, William Hebgen Guss, Alex Nichol, Alex Paino, Nikolas Tezak, Jie Tang, Igor Babuschkin, Suchir Balaji, Shantanu Jain, William Saunders, Christopher Hesse, Andrew N. Carr, Jan Leike, Josh Achiam, Vedant Misra, Evan Morikawa, Alec Radford, Matthew Knight, Miles Brundage, Mira Murati, Katie Mayer, Peter Welinder, Bob McGrew, Dario Amodei, Sam McCandlish, Ilya Sutskever, and Wojciech Zaremba. 2021. Evaluating Large Language Models Trained on Code. *arXiv preprint arXiv:2107.03374*.

Wenhu Chen, William W. Cohen, Michiel de Jong, Nitish Gupta, Alessandro Presta, Pat Verga, and John Wieting. 2022b. Qa is the new kr: Question-answer pairs as knowledge bases. *ArXiv*, abs/2207.00630.

Wenhu Chen, Hongmin Wang, Jianshu Chen, Yunkai Zhang, Hong Wang, Shiyang Li, Xiyou Zhou, and William Yang Wang. 2020a. Tabfact: A large-scale dataset for table-based fact verification. In *International Conference on Learning Representations*.

Wenhu Chen, Hanwen Zha, Zhiyu Chen, Wenhan Xiong, Hong Wang, and William Yang Wang. 2020b. HybridQA: A dataset of multi-hop question answering over tabular and textual data. In *Findings of the Association for Computational Linguistics: EMNLP 2020*, pages 1026–1036, Online. Association for Computational Linguistics.

Xinyun Chen, Chen Liang, Adams Wei Yu, Denny Zhou, Dawn Song, and Quoc V Le. 2019b. Neural symbolic reader: Scalable integration of distributed and symbolic representations for reading comprehension. In *International Conference on Learning Representations*.

Zhoujun Cheng, Tianbao Xie, Peng Shi, Chengzu Li, Rahul Nadkarni, Yushi Hu, Caiming Xiong, Dragomir Radev, Mari Ostendorf, Luke Zettlemoyer, Noah A. Smith, and Tao Yu. 2022. Binding language models in symbolic languages. *ArXiv*.

Aakanksha Chowdhery, Sharan Narang, Jacob Devlin, Maarten Bosma, Gaurav Mishra, Adam Roberts, Paul Barham, Hyung Won Chung, Charles Sutton, Sebastian Gehrmann, Parker Schuh, Kensen Shi, Sasha Tsvyashchenko, Joshua Maynez, Abhishek Rao, Parker Barnes, Yi Tay, Noam Shazeer, Vinodkumar Prabhakaran, Emily Reif, Nan Du, Ben Hutchinson, Reiner Pope, James Bradbury, Jacob Austin, Michael Isard, Guy Gur-Ari, Pengcheng Yin, Toju Duke, Anselm Levskaya, Sanjay Ghemawat, Sunipa Dev, Henryk Michalewski, Xavier Garcia, Vedant Misra, Kevin Robinson, Liam Fedus, Denny Zhou, Daphne Ippolito, David Luan, Hyeontaek Lim, Barret Zoph, Alexander Spiridonov, Ryan Sepassi, David Dohan, Shivani Agrawal, Mark Omernick, Andrew M. Dai, Thanumalayan Sankaranarayana Pillai, Marie Pellat, Aitor Lewkowycz, Erica Moreira, Rewon Child, Oleksandr Polozov, Katherine Lee, Zongwei Zhou, Xuezhi Wang, Brennan Saeta, Mark Diaz, Orhan Firat, Michele Catasta, Jason Wei, Kathy Meier-Hellstern, Douglas Eck, Jeff Dean, Slav Petrov, and Noah Fiedel. 2022. PaLM: Scaling Language Modeling with Pathways. *arXiv preprint arXiv:2204.02311*.

Karl Cobbe, Vineet Kosaraju, Mohammad Bavarian, Jacob Hilton, Reiichiro Nakano, Christopher Hesse, and John Schulman. 2021. Training verifiers to solve math word problems. *arXiv preprint arXiv:2110.14168*.

Abhishek Das, Georgia Gkioxari, Stefan Lee, Devi Parikh, and Dhruv Batra. 2018. Neural modular control for embodied question answering. In *Conference on Robot Learning*, pages 53–62. PMLR.

Pradeep Dasigi, Nelson F. Liu, Ana Marasović, Noah A. Smith, and Matt Gardner. 2019. Quoref: A reading comprehension dataset with questions requiring coreferential reasoning. In *Proceedings of the 2019 Conference on Empirical Methods in Natural Language Processing and the 9th International Joint Conference on Natural Language Processing (EMNLP-IJCNLP)*, pages 5925–5932, Hong Kong, China. Association for Computational Linguistics.

Jacob Devlin, Ming-Wei Chang, Kenton Lee, and Kristina Toutanova. 2019. BERT: Pre-training of deep bidirectional transformers for language understanding. In *Proceedings of the 2019 Conference of the North American Chapter of the Association for Computational Linguistics: Human Language Technologies, Volume 1 (Long and Short Papers)*, pages 4171–4186, Minneapolis, Minnesota. Association for Computational Linguistics.

Jay DeYoung, Sarthak Jain, Nazneen Fatema Rajani, Eric Lehman, Caiming Xiong, Richard Socher, and Byron C. Wallace. 2020. ERASER: A benchmark to evaluate rationalized NLP models. In *Proceedings of the 58th Annual Meeting of the Association for Computational Linguistics*, pages 4443–4458, Online. Association for Computational Linguistics.

Bhuwan Dhingra, Manzil Zaheer, Vidhisha Balachandran, Graham Neubig, Ruslan Salakhutdinov, and William W. Cohen. 2020. Differentiable reasoning over a virtual knowledge base. In *International Conference on Learning Representations*.

Dheeru Dua, Yizhong Wang, Pradeep Dasigi, Gabriel Stanovsky, Sameer Singh, and Matt Gardner. 2019. DROP: A reading comprehension benchmark requiring discrete reasoning over paragraphs. In *Proceedings of the 2019 Conference of the North American Chapter of the Association for Computational Linguistics: Human Language Technologies, Volume 1 (Long and Short Papers)*, pages 2368–2378, Minneapolis, Minnesota. Association for Computational Linguistics.

Yanai Elazar, Hongming Zhang, Yoav Goldberg, and Dan Roth. 2021. Back to square one: Artifact detection, training and commonsense disentanglement in the Winograd schema. In *Proceedings of the 2021 Conference on Empirical Methods in Natural Language Processing*, pages 10486–10500, Online and Punta Cana, Dominican Republic. Association for Computational Linguistics.

Yuwei Fang, Siqi Sun, Zhe Gan, Rohit Pillai, Shuohang Wang, and Jingjing Liu. 2020. Hierarchical graph network for multi-hop question answering. In *Proceedings of the 2020 Conference on Empirical Methods in Natural Language Processing (EMNLP)*, pages 8823–8838, Online. Association for Computational Linguistics.

Yanlin Feng, Xinyue Chen, Bill Yuchen Lin, Peifeng Wang, Jun Yan, and Xiang Ren. 2020. Scalable multi-hop relational reasoning for knowledge-aware question answering. In *Proceedings of the 2020 Conference on Empirical Methods in Natural Language Processing (EMNLP)*, pages 1295–1309, Online. Association for Computational Linguistics.

James Ferguson, Matt Gardner, Hannaneh Hajishirzi, Tushar Khot, and Pradeep Dasigi. 2020. IIRC: A dataset of incomplete information reading comprehension questions. In *Proceedings of the 2020 Conference on Empirical Methods in Natural Language Processing (EMNLP)*, pages 1137–1147, Online. Association for Computational Linguistics.

Luyu Gao, Aman Madaan, Shuyan Zhou, Uri Alon, Pengfei Liu, Yiming Yang, Jamie Callan, and Graham Neubig. 2022. Pal: Program-aided language models. *arXiv preprint arXiv:2211.10435*.

Mor Geva, Yoav Goldberg, and Jonathan Berant. 2019. Are we modeling the task or the annotator? an investigation of annotator bias in natural language understanding datasets. In *Proceedings of the 2019 Conference on Empirical Methods in Natural Language Processing and the 9th International Joint Conference on Natural Language Processing (EMNLP-IJCNLP)*, pages 1161–1166, Hong Kong, China. Association for Computational Linguistics.

Mor Geva, Daniel Khashabi, Elad Segal, Tushar Khot, Dan Roth, and Jonathan Berant. 2021. Did aristotle use a laptop? a question answering benchmark with implicit reasoning strategies. *Transactions of the Association for Computational Linguistics*, 9:346–361.

Max Glockner, Ivan Habernal, and Iryna Gurevych. 2020. Why do you think that? exploring faithful sentence-level rationales without supervision. In *Findings of the Association for Computational Linguistics: EMNLP 2020*, pages 1080–1095, Online. Association for Computational Linguistics.

Dirk Groeneveld, Tushar Khot, Mausam, and Ashish Sabharwal. 2020. A simple yet strong pipeline for HotpotQA. In *Proceedings of the 2020 Conference on Empirical Methods in Natural Language Processing (EMNLP)*, pages 8839–8845, Online. Association for Computational Linguistics.

Nitish Gupta, Kevin Lin, Dan Roth, Sameer Singh, and Matt Gardner. 2019. Neural module networks for reasoning over text. *arXiv preprint arXiv:1912.04971*.

Kelvin Guu, Kenton Lee, Zora Tung, Panupong Pasupat, and Ming-Wei Chang. 2020. Realm: Retrieval-augmented language model pre-training. In *International Conference on Machine Learning (ICML)*.

Bin He, Di Zhou, Jinghui Xiao, Xin Jiang, Qun Liu, Nicholas Jing Yuan, and Tong Xu. 2020. Integrating graph contextualized knowledge into pre-trained language models. In *Findings of EMNLP*.

Xanh Ho, Anh-Khoa Duong Nguyen, Saku Sugawara, and Akiko Aizawa. 2020. Constructing a multi-hop QA dataset for comprehensive evaluation of reasoning steps. In *Proceedings of the 28th International Conference on Computational Linguistics*, pages 6609–6625, Barcelona, Spain (Online). International Committee on Computational Linguistics.

Mandar Joshi, Danqi Chen, Yinhan Liu, Daniel S. Weld, Luke Zettlemoyer, and Omer Levy. 2020. SpanBERT: Improving pre-training by representing and predicting spans. *Transactions of the Association for Computational Linguistics*, 8:64–77.

Vladimir Karpukhin, Barlas Oguz, Sewon Min, Patrick Lewis, Ledell Wu, Sergey Edunov, Danqi Chen, and Wen-tau Yih. 2020. Dense passage retrieval for open-domain question answering. In *Proceedings of the 2020 Conference on Empirical Methods in Natural Language Processing (EMNLP)*, pages 6769–6781, Online. Association for Computational Linguistics.

Pei Ke, Haozhe Ji, Yu Ran, Xin Cui, Liwei Wang, Linfeng Song, Xiaoyan Zhu, and Minlie Huang. 2021. Jointgt: Graph-text joint representation learning for text generation from knowledge graphs. In *Findings of ACL*.

Tushar Khot, Peter Clark, Michal Guerquin, Peter Jansen, and Ashish Sabharwal. 2020. Qasc: A dataset for question answering via sentence composition. *Proceedings of the AAAI Conference on Artificial Intelligence*, 34(05):8082–8090.

Tushar Khot, Daniel Khashabi, Kyle Richardson, Peter Clark, and Ashish Sabharwal. 2021. Text modular networks: Learning to decompose tasks in the language of existing models. In *Proceedings of the 2021 Conference of the North American Chapter of the Association for Computational Linguistics: Human Language Technologies*, pages 1264–1279.

Tom Kwiatkowski, Jennimaria Palomaki, Olivia Redfield, Michael Collins, Ankur Parikh, Chris Alberti, Danielle Epstein, Illia Polosukhin, Jacob Devlin, Kenton Lee, Kristina Toutanova, Llion Jones, Matthew Kelcey, Ming-Wei Chang, Andrew M. Dai, Jakob Uszkoreit, Quoc Le, and Slav Petrov. 2019. Natural questions: A benchmark for question answering research. *Transactions of the Association for Computational Linguistics*, 7:452–466.

Teven Le Scao and Alexander Rush. 2021. How many data points is a prompt worth? In *Proceedings of the 2021 Conference of the North American Chapter of the Association for Computational Linguistics: Human Language Technologies*, pages 2627–2636, Online. Association for Computational Linguistics.

Tao Lei, Regina Barzilay, and Tommi Jaakkola. 2016. Rationalizing neural predictions. In *Proceedings of the 2016 Conference on Empirical Methods in Natural Language Processing*, pages 107–117, Austin, Texas. Association for Computational Linguistics.

Mike Lewis, Marjan Ghazvininejad, Gargi Ghosh, Armen Aghajanyan, Sida Wang, and Luke Zettlemoyer. 2020a. Pre-training via paraphrasing. In *Advances in Neural Information Processing Systems (NeurIPS)*.

Patrick Lewis, Ethan Perez, Aleksandra Piktus, Fabio Petroni, Vladimir Karpukhin, Naman Goyal, Heinrich Küttler, Mike Lewis, Wen-tau Yih, Tim Rocktäschel, et al. 2020b. Retrieval-augmented generation for knowledge-intensive nlp tasks. *Advances in Neural Information Processing Systems*, 33:9459–9474.

Chen Liang, Jonathan Berant, Quoc Le, Kenneth D. Forbus, and Ni Lao. 2017. Neural symbolic machines: Learning semantic parsers on Freebase with weak supervision. In *Proceedings of the 55th Annual Meeting of the Association for Computational Linguistics (Volume 1: Long Papers)*, Vancouver, Canada. Association for Computational Linguistics.

Bill Yuchen Lin, Xinyue Chen, Jamin Chen, and Xiang Ren. 2019. KagNet: Knowledge-aware graph networks for commonsense reasoning. In *Proceedings of the 2019 Conference on Empirical Methods in Natural Language Processing and the 9th International Joint Conference on Natural Language Processing (EMNLP-IJCNLP)*, pages 2829–2839, Hong Kong, China. Association for Computational Linguistics.

Bill Yuchen Lin, Haitian Sun, Bhuwan Dhingra, Manzil Zaheer, Xiang Ren, and William Cohen. 2021. Differentiable open-ended commonsense reasoning. In *Proceedings of the 2021 Conference of the North American Chapter of the Association for Computational Linguistics: Human Language Technologies*, pages 4611–4625, Online. Association for Computational Linguistics.

Bill Yuchen Lin, Kangmin Tan, Chris Miller, Beiwen Tian, and Xiang Ren. 2022. Unsupervised cross-task generalization via retrieval augmentation. *ArXiv*, abs/2204.07937.

Bill Yuchen Lin, Wangchunshu Zhou, Ming Shen, Pei Zhou, Chandra Bhagavatula, Yejin Choi, and Xiang Ren. 2020. CommonGen: A constrained text generation challenge for generative commonsense reasoning. In *Findings of the Association for Computational Linguistics: EMNLP 2020*, pages 1823–1840, Online. Association for Computational Linguistics.

Fangyu Liu, Ehsan Shareghi, Zaiqiao Meng, Marco Basaldella, and Nigel Collier. 2021. Self-alignment pretraining for biomedical entity representations. In *North American Chapter of the Association for Computational Linguistics (NAACL)*.

Jiachang Liu, Dinghan Shen, Yizhe Zhang, Bill Dolan, Lawrence Carin, and Weizhu Chen. 2022a. What makes good in-context examples for GPT-3? In *Proceedings of Deep Learning Inside Out (DeeLIO 2022): The 3rd Workshop on Knowledge Extraction and Integration for Deep Learning Architectures*, pages 100–114, Dublin, Ireland and Online. Association for Computational Linguistics.

Pengfei Liu, Weizhe Yuan, Jinlan Fu, Zhengbao Jiang, Hiroaki Hayashi, and Graham Neubig. 2022b. Pre-train, prompt, and predict: A systematic survey of prompting methods in natural language processing. *ACM Comput. Surv.* Just Accepted.

Weijie Liu, Peng Zhou, Zhe Zhao, Zhiruo Wang, Qi Ju, Haotang Deng, and P. Wang. 2020. K-bert: Enabling language representation with knowledge graph. In *AAAI Conference on Artificial Intelligence*.

Qing Lyu, Marianna Apidianaki, and Chris Callison-Burch. 2022. Towards faithful model explanation in nlp: A survey. *arXiv preprint arXiv:2209.11326*.

Aman Madaan, Niket Tandon, Peter Clark, and Yiming Yang. 2022a. Memory-assisted prompt editing to improve GPT-3 after deployment. In *Proceedings of the 2022 Conference on Empirical Methods in Natural Language Processing*, pages 2833–2861, Abu Dhabi, United Arab Emirates. Association for Computational Linguistics.

Aman Madaan, Shuyan Zhou, Uri Alon, Yiming Yang, and Graham Neubig. 2022b. Language models of code are few-shot commonsense learners. In *Proceedings of the 2022 Conference on Empirical Methods in Natural Language Processing*, pages 1384–1403, Abu Dhabi, United Arab Emirates. Association for Computational Linguistics.

Gary Marcus. 2022. Experiments Testing GPT-3's Ability at Commonsense Reasoning: Results. Accessed: 2022-08-15.

Sewon Min, Eric Wallace, Sameer Singh, Matt Gardner, Hannaneh Hajishirzi, and Luke Zettlemoyer. 2019. Compositional questions do not necessitate multi-hop reasoning. In *Proceedings of the 57th Annual Meeting of the Association for Computational Linguistics*, pages 4249–4257, Florence, Italy. Association for Computational Linguistics.

Swaroop Mishra, Daniel Khashabi, Chitta Baral, Yejin Choi, and Hannaneh Hajishirzi. 2021. Reframing Instructional Prompts to GPTk's Language. *arXiv preprint arXiv:2109.07830*.

Yasumasa Onoe, Michael Zhang, Eunsol Choi, and Greg Durrett. 2021. Creak: A dataset for commonsense reasoning over entity knowledge. In *Proceedings of the Neural Information Processing Systems Track on Datasets and Benchmarks*, volume 1.

Mihir Parmar, Swaroop Mishra, Mor Geva, and Chitta Baral. 2022. Don't blame the annotator: Bias already starts in the annotation instructions. *arXiv preprint arXiv:2205.00415*.

Panupong Pasupat and Percy Liang. 2015. Compositional semantic parsing on semi-structured tables. In *Proceedings of the 53rd Annual Meeting of the Association for Computational Linguistics and the 7th International Joint Conference on Natural Language Processing (Volume 1: Long Papers)*, pages 1470–1480, Beijing, China. Association for Computational Linguistics.

Colin Raffel, Noam Shazeer, Adam Roberts, Katherine Lee, Sharan Narang, Michael Matena, Yanqi Zhou, Wei Li, and Peter J. Liu. 2020. Exploring the limits of transfer learning with a unified text-to-text transformer. *JLMR*, 21.

Anna Rogers, Matt Gardner, and Isabelle Augenstein. 2022. Qa dataset explosion: A taxonomy of nlp resources for question answering and reading comprehension. *ACM Comput. Surv.* Just Accepted.

Corby Rosset, Chenyan Xiong, Minh Phan, Xia Song, Paul Bennett, and Saurabh Tiwary. 2020. Knowledge-aware language model pretraining. *arXiv preprint arXiv:2007.00655*.

Rachel Rudinger, Vered Shwartz, Jena D. Hwang, Chandra Bhagavatula, Maxwell Forbes, Ronan Le Bras, Noah A. Smith, and Yejin Choi. 2020. Thinking like a skeptic: Defeasible inference in natural language. In *Findings of the Association for Computational Linguistics: EMNLP 2020*, pages 4661–4675, Online. Association for Computational Linguistics.

Swarnadeep Saha, Prateek Yadav, Lisa Bauer, and Mohit Bansal. 2021. ExplaGraphs: An explanation graph generation task for structured commonsense reasoning. In *Proceedings of the 2021 Conference on Empirical Methods in Natural Language Processing*, pages 7716–7740, Online and Punta Cana, Dominican Republic. Association for Computational Linguistics.

Maarten Sap, Hannah Rashkin, Derek Chen, Ronan Le Bras, and Yejin Choi. 2019. Social IQa: Commonsense reasoning about social interactions. In *Proceedings of the 2019 Conference on Empirical Methods in Natural Language Processing and the 9th International Joint Conference on Natural Language Processing (EMNLP-IJCNLP)*, pages 4463–4473, Hong Kong, China. Association for Computational Linguistics.

Timo Schick, Jane Dwivedi-Yu, Roberto Dessì, Roberta Raileanu, Maria Lomeli, Luke Zettlemoyer, Nicola Cancedda, and Thomas Scialom. 2023. Toolformer: Language models can teach themselves to use tools. *ArXiv*, abs/2302.04761.

Tao Shen, Yi Mao, Pengcheng He, Guodong Long, Adam Trischler, and Weizhu Chen. 2020. Exploiting structured knowledge in text via graph-guided representation learning. In *Empirical Methods in Natural Language Processing (EMNLP)*.

Qi Shi, Yu Zhang, Qingyu Yin, and Ting Liu. 2021. Logic-level evidence retrieval and graph-based verification network for table-based fact verification. In *Proceedings of the 2021 Conference on Empirical Methods in Natural Language Processing*, pages 175–184, Online and Punta Cana, Dominican Republic. Association for Computational Linguistics.

Robyn Speer, Joshua Chin, and Catherine Havasi. 2017. Conceptnet 5.5: An open multilingual graph of general knowledge. *ArXiv*, abs/1612.03975.

Shane Storks, Qiaozi Gao, and Joyce Y. Chai. 2019. Commonsense reasoning for natural language understanding: A survey of benchmarks, resources, and approaches. *CoRR*, abs/1904.01172.

Tianxiang Sun, Yunfan Shao, Xipeng Qiu, Qipeng Guo, Yaru Hu, Xuan-Jing Huang, and Zheng Zhang. 2020. Colake: Contextualized language and knowledge embedding. In *International Conference on Computational Linguistics (COLING)*.

Yu Sun, Shuohuan Wang, Shikun Feng, Siyu Ding, Chao Pang, Junyuan Shang, Jiaxiang Liu, Xuyi Chen, Yanbin Zhao, Yuxiang Lu, et al. 2021. Ernie 3.0: Large-scale knowledge enhanced pre-training for language understanding and generation. *arXiv preprint arXiv:2107.02137*.

Alon Talmor and Jonathan Berant. 2018. The web as a knowledge-base for answering complex questions. In *Proceedings of the 2018 Conference of the North American Chapter of the Association for Computational Linguistics: Human Language Technologies, Volume 1 (Long Papers)*, pages 641–651, New Orleans, Louisiana. Association for Computational Linguistics.

Alon Talmor, Ori Yoran, Ronan Le Bras, Chandra Bhagavatula, Yoav Goldberg, Yejin Choi, and Jonathan Berant. 2021a. CommonsenseQA 2.0: Exposing the limits of AI through gamification. In *Thirty-fifth Conference on Neural Information Processing Systems Datasets and Benchmarks Track (Round 1)*.

Alon Talmor, Ori Yoran, Amnon Catav, Dan Lahav, Yizhong Wang, Akari Asai, Gabriel Ilharco, Hannaneh Hajishirzi, and Jonathan Berant. 2021b. Multimodal{qa}: complex question answering over text, tables and images. In *International Conference on Learning Representations*.

Yixuan Tang, Hwee Tou Ng, and Anthony Tung. 2021. Do multi-hop question answering systems know how to answer the single-hop sub-questions? In *Proceedings of the 16th Conference of the European Chapter of the Association for Computational Linguistics: Main Volume*, pages 3244–3249, Online. Association for Computational Linguistics.

James Thorne, Majid Yazdani, Marzieh Saeidi, Fabrizio Silvestri, Sebastian Riedel, and Alon Halevy. 2021. Database reasoning over text. *arXiv preprint arXiv:2106.01074*.

Harsh Trivedi, Niranjan Balasubramanian, Tushar Khot, and Ashish Sabharwal. 2022. MuSiQue: Multi-hop questions via single-hop question composition. *Transactions of the Association for Computational Linguistics*, 10:539–554.

Ming Tu, Guangtao Wang, Jing Huang, Yun Tang, Xiaodong He, and Bowen Zhou. 2019. Multi-hop reading comprehension across multiple documents by reasoning over heterogeneous graphs. In *Proceedings of the 57th Annual Meeting of the Association for Computational Linguistics*, pages 2704–2713, Florence, Italy. Association for Computational Linguistics.

Xiaozhi Wang, Tianyu Gao, Zhaocheng Zhu, Zhengyan Zhang, Zhiyuan Liu, Juanzi Li, and Jian Tang. 2021. Kepler: A unified model for knowledge embedding and pre-trained language representation. *Transactions of the Association for Computational Linguistics (TACL)*.

Jason Wei, Xuezhi Wang, Dale Schuurmans, Maarten Bosma, Ed Chi, Quoc Le, and Denny Zhou. 2022a. Chain of thought prompting elicits reasoning in large language models. *arXiv preprint arXiv:2201.11903*.

Jason Wei, Xuezhi Wang, Dale Schuurmans, Maarten Bosma, Ed Chi, Quoc Le, and Denny Zhou. 2022b. Chain of Thought Prompting Elicits Reasoning in Large Language Models. *arXiv preprint arXiv:2201.11903*.

Jason Wei, Xuezhi Wang, Dale Schuurmans, Maarten Bosma, Ed Chi, Quoc Le, and Denny Zhou. 2022c. Chain of Thought Prompting Elicits Reasoning in Large Language Models. *arXiv preprint arXiv:2201.11903*.

Sarah Wiegreffe and Ana Marasović. 2021. Teach me to explain: A review of datasets for explainable nlp. In *Proceedings of NeurIPS*.

Tomer Wolfson, Mor Geva, Ankit Gupta, Matt Gardner, Yoav Goldberg, Daniel Deutch, and Jonathan Berant. 2020. Break it down: A question understanding benchmark. *Transactions of the Association for Computational Linguistics*.

Tianbao Xie, Chen Henry Wu, Peng Shi, Ruiqi Zhong, Torsten Scholak, Michihiro Yasunaga, Chien-Sheng Wu, Ming Zhong, Pengcheng Yin, Sida I. Wang, Victor Zhong, Bailin Wang, Chengzu Li, Connor Boyle, Ansong Ni, Ziyu Yao, Dragomir Radev, Caiming Xiong, Lingpeng Kong, Rui Zhang, Noah A. Smith, Luke Zettlemoyer, and Tao Yu. 2022. Unifiedskg: Unifying and multi-tasking structured knowledge grounding with text-to-text language models. *EMNLP*.

Wenhan Xiong, Jingfei Du, William Yang Wang, and Veselin Stoyanov. 2020. Pretrained encyclopedia: Weakly supervised knowledge-pretrained language model. In *International Conference on Learning Representations (ICLR)*.

Zhilin Yang, Peng Qi, Saizheng Zhang, Yoshua Bengio, William Cohen, Ruslan Salakhutdinov, and Christopher D. Manning. 2018. HotpotQA: A dataset for diverse, explainable multi-hop question answering. In *Proceedings of the 2018 Conference on Empirical Methods in Natural Language Processing*, pages 2369–2380, Brussels, Belgium. Association for Computational Linguistics.

Michihiro Yasunaga, Antoine Bosselut, Hongyu Ren, Xikun Zhang, Christopher D. Manning, Percy Liang, and Jure Leskovec. 2022a. Deep bidirectional language-knowledge graph pretraining. In *Neural Information Processing Systems (NeurIPS)*.

Michihiro Yasunaga, Jure Leskovec, and Percy Liang. 2022b. LinkBERT: Pretraining language models with document links. In *Proceedings of the 60th Annual Meeting of the Association for Computational Linguistics (Volume 1: Long Papers)*, pages 8003–8016, Dublin, Ireland. Association for Computational Linguistics.

Michihiro Yasunaga, Hongyu Ren, Antoine Bosselut, Percy Liang, and Jure Leskovec. 2021. QA-GNN: Reasoning with language models and knowledge graphs for question answering. In *Proceedings of the 2021 Conference of the North American Chapter of the Association for Computational Linguistics: Human Language Technologies*, pages 535–546, Online. Association for Computational Linguistics.

Donghan Yu, Chenguang Zhu, Yiming Yang, and Michael Zeng. 2022a. Jaket: Joint pre-training of knowledge graph and language understanding. In *AAAI Conference on Artificial Intelligence*.

Tao Yu, Rui Zhang, Kai Yang, Michihiro Yasunaga, Dongxu Wang, Zifan Li, James Ma, Irene Li, Qingning Yao, Shanelle Roman, Zilin Zhang, and Dragomir Radev. 2018. Spider: A large-scale human-labeled dataset for complex and cross-domain semantic parsing and text-to-sql task. In *Proceedings of the 2018 Conference on Empirical Methods in Natural Language Processing*, Brussels, Belgium. Association for Computational Linguistics.

W. Yu, Chenguang Zhu, Zhihan Zhang, Shuohang Wang, Zhuosheng Zhang, Yuwei Fang, and Meng Jiang. 2022b. Retrieval augmentation for commonsense reasoning: A unified approach. *ArXiv*, abs/2210.12887.

Luke S. Zettlemoyer and Michael Collins. 2005. Learning to map sentences to logical form: Structured classification with probabilistic categorial grammars. *UAI*.

Susan Zhang, Stephen Roller, Naman Goyal, Mikel Artetxe, Moya Chen, Shuohui Chen, Christopher Dewan, Mona Diab, Xian Li, Xi Victoria Lin, et al. 2022a. Opt: Open pre-trained transformer language models. *arXiv preprint arXiv:2205.01068*.

Xikun Zhang, Antoine Bosselut, Michihiro Yasunaga, Hongyu Ren, Percy Liang, Christopher D Manning, and Jure Leskovec. 2022b. GreaseLM: Graph REASoning enhanced language models. In *International Conference on Learning Representations*.

Zhengyan Zhang, Xu Han, Zhiyuan Liu, Xin Jiang, Maosong Sun, and Qun Liu. 2019. Ernie: Enhanced language representation with informative entities. In *Association for Computational Linguistics (ACL)*.

Hattie Zhou, Azade Nova, Hugo Larochelle, Aaron Courville, Behnam Neyshabur, and Hanie Sedghi. 2022. Teaching algorithmic reasoning via in-context learning. *arXiv preprint arXiv:2211.09066*.

Wangchunshu Zhou, Jinyi Hu, Hanlin Zhang, Xiaodan Liang, Maosong Sun, Chenyan Xiong, and Jian Tang. 2020. Towards interpretable natural language understanding with explanations as latent variables. *Advances in Neural Information Processing Systems*, 33:6803–6814.

Zhaocheng Zhu, Mikhail Galkin, Zuobai Zhang, and Jian Tang. 2022. Neural-symbolic models for logical queries on knowledge graphs. *arXiv preprint arXiv:2205.10128*.

ACL/EACL/EMNLP 2023 Tutorial Proposal
Everything you need to know about Multilingual LLMs: Towards fair, performant and reliable models for the languages of the world

Sunayana Sitaram
Microsoft Research India
sunayana,sitaram@microsoft.com

Monojit Choudhury
Microsoft Turing, India
monojitc@microsoft.com

Barun Patra
Microsoft Turing, USA
bapatra@microsoft.com

Vishrav Chaudhary
Microsoft Turing, USA
vchaudhary@microsoft.com

Kabir Ahuja
Microsoft Research India
t-kabirahuja@microsoft.com

Kalika Bali
Microsoft Research India
kalikab@microsoft.com

1 Tutorial content

This tutorial will describe various aspects of scaling up language technologies to many of the world's languages by presenting the latest research in Massively Multilingual Language Models (MMLMs). We will cover topics such as data collection, training and fine-tuning of models, Responsible AI issues such as fairness, bias and toxicity, linguistic diversity and evaluation in the context of MMLMs, specifically focusing on issues in non-English and low-resource languages. Further, we will also talk about some of the real-world challenges in deploying these models in language communities in the field. With the performance of MMLMs improving in the zero-shot setting for many languages, it is now becoming feasible to use them for building language technologies in many languages of the world, and this tutorial will provide the computational linguistics community with unique insights from the latest research in multilingual models. Although past tutorials have covered some of these topics (such as linguistic diversity, data and training of models), there has been a lot of interesting research in the recent past that the CL community will benefit from knowing about. Further, this will be the first tutorial (as per our knowledge) that will discuss issues of deployment in language communities and Responsible AI in the context of multilingual models.

This tutorial will present a broad survey covering work done by several research groups (as indicated in the references), including work done by the authors.

Type of the tutorial: cutting-edge

Target audience and pre-requisites: The target audience for this tutorial are researchers from industry and academia who work on Large Language Models, and are interested in learning about the latest research in multilingual models to build systems for non-English languages, low-resource languages and multilingual speakers. We will not be covering the basics of LLMs, so we expect that the audience will be familiar with (at least the English versions of) models such as BERT.

1.1 Outline of the tutorial

We plan to have five talks of 30/40 minutes each, along with a 10 minute introduction, with 10 minutes for general discussion/spillover.

Introduction: We will start with a short introduction on MMLMs, describing the models that are available today and present the SOTA in model performance on various tasks across different languages.

Data and pre-training: The main goal of this section would be to outline the techniques leveraged for creating a high quality corpus for pre-training strong MMLMs. We will cover the challenges encountered in creating such a corpus as highlighted in CC100 (Conneau et al., 2020), mC4 (Xue et al., 2021), OSCAR (Ortiz Suárez et al., 2020), ROOTS (Laurençon et al., 2022) etc., and provide an overview of the various stages of such a dataset creation pipeline. Ensuring the quality of the training corpus is highly important as it is directly correlated to the performance of MMLMs (Kaplan et al., 2020). In addition to this, we will also discuss the pre-training strategies and possible extensions for extending the recipe to multiple languages (Conneau and Lample, 2019; Artetxe and Schwenk, 2019) describing how scaling (both on the data and model axis) can substantially help improve model performance (Conneau et al., 2020;

Proceedings of the 61st Annual Meeting of the Association for Computational Linguistics
Volume 6: Tutorial Abstracts, pages 21–26
July 9, 2023 ©2023 Association for Computational Linguistics

Xue et al., 2021), aiding in bridging the gap between the English performance of a multilingual and an English only model, thereby reducing the curse of Multilinguality.

Training paradigms and fine-tuning: We will describe different training paradigms (Eg: an Electra based approach (Chi et al., 2022; He et al., 2021)) and how to leverage bitext data, discussing results of using contrastive learning approaches (Chi et al., 2021) or extensions to Electra based approaches (Chi et al., 2022), as well as showing the benefits of going beyond English centric bitexts (Patra et al., 2022). We will also discuss some orthogonal approaches of training encoder-decoder multilingual representation models (Liu et al., 2020; Ma et al., 2021; **?**), as well as complimentary techniques to build better encoder models (Eg: Adapter based approaches (Pfeiffer et al., 2022)). We will also focus on different strategies for improving the fine-tuning performance of these models. This includes techniques encouraging models to have more consistent predictions across languages (Zheng et al., 2021), leveraging weight perturbations to avoid overfitting (Wu et al., 2022) or techniques to reduce the sharpness of loss minima for better generalization (Foret et al., 2021; Bahri et al., 2022).

Performance evaluation and reliability: While the state-of-the-art multilingual models support around 100 languages of the world, most existing multilingual benchmarks contain evaluation data in a handful of languages (Ahuja et al., 2022b). We will discuss some potential approaches to scale up multilingual evaluation like performance prediction (Lin et al., 2019; Xia et al., 2020; Ahuja et al., 2022c) and structure probing (Müller-Eberstein et al., 2022; Clouâtre et al., 2022). We will also focus on measuring the cost-performance trade-offs and sample efficiencies of fine-tuning MMLMs with different sources of data (translation vs manual collection)(Ahuja et al., 2022a). Further, we will cover how to measure reliability in the confidence predictions of multilingual models under a zero-shot and few-shot setup by studying their calibration (Ahuja et al., 2022d).

FATE issues: LLMs are known to pick up the biases present in the datasets that are trained on. In case of multilingual LLMs, apart from bias and fairness issues at group and individual level, one also need to address the issue of disparity of zero-shot transfer accuracies across languages and varieties (Choudhury and Deshpande, 2021; Lauscher et al., 2020). Furthermore, there is little work done on the interaction among the biases in corpora from different languages, influence of grammatical gender (Cao and Daumé, 2021) and other syntactic and semantic factors on measurement and mitigation of biases, and socio-cultural aspects of biases (Sambasivan et al., 2021). In this section of the tutorial, we will survey the work done so far in non-English FATE issues and present challenges that remain to be addressed.

Deploying to language communities: LLMs today are trained using billions of parameters, making them infeasible to be used in low-memory footprint devices. Language communities (particularly those that speak under-resourced languages) that may benefit the most from Speech and NLP technologies may not have good enough connectivity to be able to use models hosted on the cloud. This necessitates the development or distillation of lightweight models for low-resource languages, and in this section, we will present research in this direction (Diddee et al., 2022). We will study the state of current LT to serve communities speaking different languages for critical situations such as healthcare bots (Mondal et al., 2022). Further, there are many social and cultural factors to be taken into account while deploying MMLMs to language communities, which we will also discuss in this section.

1.2 Diversity considerations

The topic of the tutorial inherently encourages linguistic diversity. In terms of gender diversity, two of the tutorial presenters are female, while four are male. In this tutorial, we will cover issues related to Responsible AI (fairness, toxicity) and deploying to under-resourced language communities which will improve diversity considerations while building LLMs. The instructors are a mix of senior, mid-career and junior researchers.

1.3 Reading list

Please check the references section for the reading list.

2 Instructor bios

Sunayana Sitaram is a Senior Researcher at Microsoft Research India, where she works on multilingual speech and NLP. Her current research interests include training and evaluation of Massively Multilingual Language Models and Responsible AI for NLP. Prior to coming to MSRI as a Post Doc, Sunayana completed her MS and PhD at the Language Technologies Institute, Carnegie Mellon University in 2015. Sunayana's research has been published in top NLP and Speech conferences including ACL, NAACL, EMNLP, Interspeech, ICASSP. She has organized special sessions and workshops on under-resourced languages, code-switching, multilingual evaluation and speech for social good. She has also led the creation of several benchmarks and datasets in code-switching, ASR, NLI and TTS that have been used by research groups all over the world.

Monojit Choudhury is a Principal Applied Scientist at Microsoft Turing, prior to which he was a Principal Researcher at Microsoft Research India. He is also a Professor of Practice at Plaksha University, and had held adjunct faculty positions at Ashoka University, IIIT Hyderabad and IIT Kharagpur. Over the past 15 years, Monojit has worked on several impactful projects on processing of code-mixed text, evaluation and linguistic fairness of large language models, and social impact through participatory design of technology for under-resourced languages like Gondi, Mundari, Idu Mishmi and Swahili. Monojit has served as Senior Area Chair and Area chair in leading NLP and AI conferences including EMNLP, ACL, NAACL, IJCNLP and AAAI. He has organized several successful workshops in *ACL conferences (SUMEval 2022, CALCS series, TextGraph series, etc.) and has delivered a tutorial on Code-mixed text processing at EMNLP 2019. He is the general chair of the Panini Linguistics Olympiad and the founding co-chair of Asia Pacific Linguistics Olympiad – programs to introduce bright young students to linguistics and computational linguistics through puzzles. Dr. Choudhury holds PhD and B.Tech degrees in Computer Science and Engineering from IIT Kharagpur.

Vishrav Chaudhary is a Principal Researcher at Microsoft Turing where he works on scaling and building efficient Multilingual and Multimodal representation and generation models. Prior to Microsoft, Vishrav was a Lead Researcher at FAIR and focused on several aspects of Machine Translation, Quality Estimation and Cross-lingual understanding. Over the past 10 years, Vishrav's research work has been published in several leading NLP and AI conferences and journals including ACL, EMNLP, NAACL, EACL, AACL, TACL, JMLR and AMTA. He has also organized several workshops successfully including SUMEval 2022, AmericasNLP 2021, WMT 2021 etc. He has also served as an Area Chair for EMNLP 2022. Vishrav has also led creation of benchmarks and datasets targeting 100+ languages which have been used to train state-of-the-art Cross Lingual Representation and Machine Translation models.

Barun Patra is an Applied Scientist at Microsoft Turing. His research interest revolves around building better foundational models that can help support numerous NLP tasks across different languages. Barun's research work focuses on improving the quality and efficiency of training these large multilingual foundational models, helping achieve state-of-the-art performance on cross-lingual NLP tasks.

Kabir Ahuja is a Research Fellow at Microsoft Research India, where he works on building linguistically fair multilingual models covering different aspects around their performance, calibration, evaluation, interpretation, and data collection. He is also interested in the analysis and interpretability of the computation mechanisms utilized by neural sequence models for solving different tasks.

Kalika Bali is a Principal Researcher at Microsoft Research India working in the areas of Machine Learning, Natural Language Systems and Applications, as well as Technology for Emerging Markets. Her research interests lie broadly in the area of Speech and Language Technology especially in the use of linguistic models for building technology that offers a more natural Human-Computer as well as Computer-Mediated interactions.

3 Other

Estimate of audience size: 50

Venues: We would prefer ACL 2023 to be the venue for the tutorial, but EMNLP and EACL are also acceptable. We do not forsee any special requirements for technical equipment.

3.1 Ethics statement

This tutorial will present current research on Multilingual model training, evaluation, Responsible AI issues and deploying models in the field. Although we aim to promote linguistic diversity by discussing issues pertaining to multilingual models trained on around 100 languages, many languages of the world are not supported by these models. Further, the techniques that we will discuss mainly apply to written languages, while unwritten languages will be excluded from the tutorial.

References

Kabir Ahuja, Monojit Choudhury, and Sandipan Dandapat. 2022a. On the economics of multilingual few-shot learning: Modeling the cost-performance trade-offs of machine translated and manual data. In *Proceedings of the 2022 Conference of the North American Chapter of the Association for Computational Linguistics: Human Language Technologies*, pages 1369–1384, Seattle, United States. Association for Computational Linguistics.

Kabir Ahuja, Sandipan Dandapat, Sunayana Sitaram, and Monojit Choudhury. 2022b. Beyond static models and test sets: Benchmarking the potential of pre-trained models across tasks and languages. In *Proceedings of NLP Power! The First Workshop on Efficient Benchmarking in NLP*, pages 64–74, Dublin, Ireland. Association for Computational Linguistics.

Kabir Ahuja, Shanu Kumar, Sandipan Dandapat, and Monojit Choudhury. 2022c. Multi task learning for zero shot performance prediction of multilingual models. In *Proceedings of the 60th Annual Meeting of the Association for Computational Linguistics (Volume 1: Long Papers)*, pages 5454–5467, Dublin, Ireland. Association for Computational Linguistics.

Kabir Ahuja, Sunayana Sitaram, Sandipan Dandapat, and Monojit Choudhury. 2022d. On the calibration of massively multilingual language models.

Mikel Artetxe and Holger Schwenk. 2019. Massively multilingual sentence embeddings for zero-shot cross-lingual transfer and beyond. *Transactions of the Association for Computational Linguistics*, 7:597–610.

Dara Bahri, Hossein Mobahi, and Yi Tay. 2022. Sharpness-aware minimization improves language model generalization. In *Proceedings of the 60th Annual Meeting of the Association for Computational Linguistics (Volume 1: Long Papers)*, pages 7360–7371, Dublin, Ireland. Association for Computational Linguistics.

Yang Trista Cao and III Daumé, Hal. 2021. Toward Gender-Inclusive Coreference Resolution: An Analysis of Gender and Bias Throughout the Machine Learning Lifecycle*. *Computational Linguistics*, 47(3):615–661.

Zewen Chi, Li Dong, Furu Wei, Nan Yang, Saksham Singhal, Wenhui Wang, Xia Song, Xian-Ling Mao, Heyan Huang, and Ming Zhou. 2021. InfoXLM: An information-theoretic framework for cross-lingual language model pre-training. In *Proceedings of the 2021 Conference of the North American Chapter of the Association for Computational Linguistics: Human Language Technologies*, pages 3576–3588, Online. Association for Computational Linguistics.

Zewen Chi, Shaohan Huang, Li Dong, Shuming Ma, Bo Zheng, Saksham Singhal, Payal Bajaj, Xia Song, Xian-Ling Mao, Heyan Huang, and Furu Wei. 2022. XLM-E: Cross-lingual language model pre-training via ELECTRA. In *Proceedings of the 60th Annual Meeting of the Association for Computational Linguistics (Volume 1: Long Papers)*, pages 6170–6182, Dublin, Ireland. Association for Computational Linguistics.

Monojit Choudhury and Amit Deshpande. 2021. How linguistically fair are multilingual pre-trained language models? *Proceedings of the AAAI Conference on Artificial Intelligence*, 35(14):12710–12718.

Louis Clouâtre, Prasanna Parthasarathi, Amal Zouaq, and Sarath Chandar. 2022. Detecting languages unintelligible to multilingual models through local structure probes.

Alexis Conneau, Kartikay Khandelwal, Naman Goyal, Vishrav Chaudhary, Guillaume Wenzek, Francisco Guzmán, Edouard Grave, Myle Ott, Luke Zettlemoyer, and Veselin Stoyanov. 2020. Unsupervised cross-lingual representation learning at scale. In *Proceedings of the 58th Annual Meeting of the Association for Computational Linguistics*, pages 8440–8451, Online. Association for Computational Linguistics.

Alexis Conneau and Guillaume Lample. 2019. Cross-lingual language model pretraining. In *Advances in Neural Information Processing Systems*, volume 32. Curran Associates, Inc.

Harshita Diddee, Sandipan Dandapat, Monojit Choudhury, Tanuja Ganu, and Kalika Bali. 2022. Too brittle to touch: Comparing the stability of quantization and distillation towards developing lightweight low-resource mt models.

Pierre Foret, Ariel Kleiner, Hossein Mobahi, and Behnam Neyshabur. 2021. Sharpness-aware minimization for efficiently improving generalization. In *International Conference on Learning Representations*.

Pengcheng He, Jianfeng Gao, and Weizhu Chen. 2021. Debertav3: Improving deberta using electra-style pre-training with gradient-disentangled embedding sharing. *arXiv preprint arXiv:2111.09543*.

Jared Kaplan, Sam McCandlish, Tom Henighan, Tom B. Brown, Benjamin Chess, Rewon Child, Scott Gray, Alec Radford, Jeffrey Wu, and Dario Amodei. 2020. Scaling laws for neural language models. *CoRR*, abs/2001.08361.

Hugo Laurençon, Lucile Saulnier, Thomas Wang, Christopher Akiki, Albert Villanova del Moral, Teven Le Scao, Leandro Von Werra, Chenghao Mou, Eduardo González Ponferrada, Huu Nguyen, Jörg

Frohberg, Mario Šaško, Quentin Lhoest, Angelina McMillan-Major, Gérard Dupont, Stella Biderman, Anna Rogers, Loubna Ben allal, Francesco De Toni, Giada Pistilli, Olivier Nguyen, Somaieh Nikpoor, Maraim Masoud, Pierre Colombo, Javier de la Rosa, Paulo Villegas, Tristan Thrush, Shayne Longpre, Sebastian Nagel, Leon Weber, Manuel Romero Muñoz, Jian Zhu, Daniel Van Strien, Zaid Alyafeai, Khalid Almubarak, Vu Minh Chien, Itziar Gonzalez-Dios, Aitor Soroa, Kyle Lo, Manan Dey, Pedro Ortiz Suarez, Aaron Gokaslan, Shamik Bose, David Ifeoluwa Adelani, Long Phan, Hieu Tran, Ian Yu, Suhas Pai, Jenny Chim, Violette Lepercq, Suzana Ilic, Margaret Mitchell, Sasha Luccioni, and Yacine Jernite. 2022. The bigscience ROOTS corpus: A 1.6TB composite multilingual dataset. In *Thirty-sixth Conference on Neural Information Processing Systems Datasets and Benchmarks Track*.

Anne Lauscher, Vinit Ravishankar, Ivan Vulić, and Goran Glavaš. 2020. From zero to hero: On the limitations of zero-shot language transfer with multilingual Transformers. In *Proceedings of the 2020 Conference on Empirical Methods in Natural Language Processing (EMNLP)*, pages 4483–4499, Online. Association for Computational Linguistics.

Yu-Hsiang Lin, Chian-Yu Chen, Jean Lee, Zirui Li, Yuyan Zhang, Mengzhou Xia, Shruti Rijhwani, Junxian He, Zhisong Zhang, Xuezhe Ma, Antonios Anastasopoulos, Patrick Littell, and Graham Neubig. 2019. Choosing transfer languages for cross-lingual learning. In *Proceedings of the 57th Annual Meeting of the Association for Computational Linguistics*, pages 3125–3135, Florence, Italy. Association for Computational Linguistics.

Yinhan Liu, Jiatao Gu, Naman Goyal, Xian Li, Sergey Edunov, Marjan Ghazvininejad, Mike Lewis, and Luke Zettlemoyer. 2020. Multilingual denoising pretraining for neural machine translation. *Transactions of the Association for Computational Linguistics*, 8:726–742.

Shuming Ma, Li Dong, Shaohan Huang, Dongdong Zhang, Alexandre Muzio, Saksham Singhal, Hany Hassan Awadalla, Xia Song, and Furu Wei. 2021. Deltalm: Encoder-decoder pre-training for language generation and translation by augmenting pretrained multilingual encoders. *arXiv preprint arXiv:2106.13736*.

Ishani Mondal, Kabir Ahuja, Mohit Jain, Jacki O'Neill, Kalika Bali, and Monojit Choudhury. 2022. Global readiness of language technology for healthcare: What would it take to combat the next pandemic? In *Proceedings of the 29th International Conference on Computational Linguistics*, pages 4320–4335, Gyeongju, Republic of Korea. International Committee on Computational Linguistics.

Max Müller-Eberstein, Rob van der Goot, and Barbara Plank. 2022. Sort by structure: Language model ranking as dependency probing. In *Proceedings of the 2022 Conference of the North American Chapter of the Association for Computational Linguistics: Human Language Technologies*, pages 1296–1307, Seattle, United States. Association for Computational Linguistics.

Pedro Javier Ortiz Suárez, Laurent Romary, and Benoît Sagot. 2020. A monolingual approach to contextualized word embeddings for mid-resource languages. In *Proceedings of the 58th Annual Meeting of the Association for Computational Linguistics*, pages 1703–1714, Online. Association for Computational Linguistics.

Barun Patra, Saksham Singhal, Shaohan Huang, Zewen Chi, Li Dong, Furu Wei, Vishrav Chaudhary, and Xia Song. 2022. Beyond english-centric bitexts for better multilingual language representation learning. *arXiv preprint arXiv:2210.14867*.

Jonas Pfeiffer, Naman Goyal, Xi Lin, Xian Li, James Cross, Sebastian Riedel, and Mikel Artetxe. 2022. Lifting the curse of multilinguality by pre-training modular transformers. In *Proceedings of the 2022 Conference of the North American Chapter of the Association for Computational Linguistics: Human Language Technologies*, pages 3479–3495, Seattle, United States. Association for Computational Linguistics.

Nithya Sambasivan, Erin Arnesen, Ben Hutchinson, Tulsee Doshi, and Vinodkumar Prabhakaran. 2021. Re-imagining algorithmic fairness in india and beyond. In *Proceedings of the 2021 ACM Conference on Fairness, Accountability, and Transparency*, FAccT '21, page 315–328, New York, NY, USA. Association for Computing Machinery.

Chuhan Wu, Fangzhao Wu, Tao Qi, and Yongfeng Huang. 2022. NoisyTune: A little noise can help you finetune pretrained language models better. In *Proceedings of the 60th Annual Meeting of the Association for Computational Linguistics (Volume 2: Short Papers)*, pages 680–685, Dublin, Ireland. Association for Computational Linguistics.

Mengzhou Xia, Antonios Anastasopoulos, Ruochen Xu, Yiming Yang, and Graham Neubig. 2020. Predicting performance for natural language processing tasks. In *Proceedings of the 58th Annual Meeting of the Association for Computational Linguistics*, pages 8625–8646, Online. Association for Computational Linguistics.

Linting Xue, Noah Constant, Adam Roberts, Mihir Kale, Rami Al-Rfou, Aditya Siddhant, Aditya Barua, and Colin Raffel. 2021. mT5: A massively multilingual pre-trained text-to-text transformer. In *Proceedings of the 2021 Conference of the North American Chapter of the Association for Computational Linguistics: Human Language Technologies*, pages 483–498, Online. Association for Computational Linguistics.

Bo Zheng, Li Dong, Shaohan Huang, Wenhui Wang, Zewen Chi, Saksham Singhal, Wanxiang Che, Ting

Liu, Xia Song, and Furu Wei. 2021. Consistency regularization for cross-lingual fine-tuning. In *Proceedings of the 59th Annual Meeting of the Association for Computational Linguistics and the 11th International Joint Conference on Natural Language Processing (Volume 1: Long Papers)*, pages 3403–3417, Online. Association for Computational Linguistics.

Generating Text from Language Models

Afra Amini[1] **Ryan Cotterell**[1] **John Hewitt**[2]
Clara Meister[1] **Tiago Pimentel**[3]
[1]ETH Zürich [2]Stanford University [3]University of Cambridge
afra.amini@inf.ethz.ch ryan.cotterell@inf.ethz.ch
johnhew@cs.stanford.edu clara.meister@inf.ethz.ch
tp472@cam.ac.uk

Abstract

An increasingly large percentage of natural language processing (NLP) tasks center around the generation of text from probabilistic language models. Despite this trend, techniques for improving or specifying preferences in these generated texts rely mostly on intuition-based heuristics. Further, there lacks a unified presentation of their motivations, practical implementation, successes and pitfalls. Practitioners must, therefore, choose somewhat blindly between generation algorithms—like top-p sampling or beam search—which can lead to wildly different results. At the same time, language generation research continues to criticize and improve the standard toolboxes, further adding entropy to the state of the field. In this tutorial, we will provide a centralized and cohesive discussion of critical considerations when choosing how to generate from a language model. We will cover a wide range of empirically-observed problems (like degradation, hallucination, repetition) and their corresponding proposed algorithmic solutions from recent research (like top-p sampling and its successors). We will then discuss a subset of these algorithms under a unified light; most stochastic generation strategies can be framed as *locally adapting* the probabilities of a model to avoid failure cases. Finally, we will then cover methods in *controlled* generation, that go beyond just ensuring coherence to ensure text exhibits specific desired properties. We aim for NLP practitioners and researchers to leave our tutorial with a unified framework which they can use to evaluate and contribute to the latest research in language generation.

1 Introduction and Motivation

With their widespread public availability, large pretrained language models have become a core part of many natural language processing (NLP) pipelines. This trend is particularly evident in language generation tasks, where prompt engineering and controlled generation techniques have shown that these models can essentially be used "out-of-the-box" for various language generation needs. Yet, as has been observed repeatedly, how one chooses to generate text from these models can lead to vastly different results; make the wrong choice and a language model can fall into repetitive loops (Welleck et al., 2020), generate gibberish (Holtzman et al., 2020), or make up random facts (Maynez et al., 2020). In the effort to circumnavigate these issues, one can make use of a variety of relatively straightforward methods: (i) sampling adapters, simple modifications to token-level distributions that help prevent the generation of incoherent text; (ii) controlled generation methods, techniques that guide these models to output strings with a set of desired attributes. While employing these methods often does not require domain expertise, many people do not have proper knowledge of the tools available—and much less how and when to apply them. Hence, without years of experience in this subfield, both NLP researchers and practitioners may have difficulty using pretrained language models for text generation, as they will likely encounter the problematic behaviors mentioned above.

In this **cutting-edge** tutorial, we aim to offer a comprehensive introduction to techniques for generating strings from language models, discussing both how to sample adeptly from and explicitly control them. This tutorial will be divided in four parts. First, we will present background knowledge on language modeling, discussing both its mathematical formulation, and the empirically-observed shortcomings of modern models. Second, we will cover the basics of language generation, presenting both deterministic and stochastic decoding strategies. Third, we present a unifying framework for sampling adapters, the family of methods often used for stochastic decoding that transform the output of a model according to qualitatively motivated rules. Finally, we will discuss several methods for controlled text generation, i.e., methods that allow

Proceedings of the 61st Annual Meeting of the Association for Computational Linguistics
Volume 6: Tutorial Abstracts, pages 27–31

users to enforce constraints on the text output by models. We believe this will equip the NLP community with the knowledge of how to better employ these models for their downstream use-cases, thus making them more broadly accessible.

2 Target Audience and Preferred Venue

Our tutorial is targeted at members of the NLP community who wish to make use of language models for various language generation tasks. This includes researchers, interested in e.g., data augmentation techniques, as well as practitioners wishing to make use of pretrained language models in their language generation pipelines. We expect that participants are comfortable with probabilistic formulations of NLP tasks, as well as the structure and formulation of standard autoregressive models e.g., transformers. While we do not require any readings, we recommend reviewing (in no particular order) the works cited in this proposal. Given the rising popularity of tasks involving language generation, we estimate an audience of approximately 100 people. We would be willing to present this tutorial at both ACL and EMNLP.

3 Outline

3.1 Part 1: Background

Modern natural language processing tends to proceed by (1) framing a task in probabilistic terms, (2) estimating a model to imitate the task's generative processes (typically using finite training datasets as a proxy), and then (3) using this generative model as a tool to accomplish the task. More precisely, practitioners take a textual dataset $\mathcal{D} = \{\mathbf{y}_n\}_{n=1}^{N}$—an N-sized set of strings over some vocabulary $\mathcal{V}$—and treat it as a set of independently and identically distributed samples from a distribution $p(\mathbf{y})$, where $\mathbf{y} \in \mathcal{V}^*$. We will use p to denote the *true* distribution—the distribution defined by the task's hypothetical generative process, from which we drew our samples.

In this tutorial, we'll focus largely on autoregressive models of p, meaning that we decompose the probability of a string as $p(\mathbf{y}) = \prod_{t=1}^{T} p(y_t \mid \mathbf{y}_{<t})$ and build a model of the conditional distribution $p(y_t \mid \mathbf{y}_{<t})$ instead. In practice, the vast majority of these models, which we denote as p_θ, are trained to minimize the empirical KL-divergence with the finite set of samples $\mathcal{D}$.

Successes and known failures. It is hard to overstate the improvements in modeling performance that have occurred in the last five years, as measured simply in terms of cross entropy. Still, language generation techniques are used both to avoid known failure modes and to coax more desirable properties out of language models. In our tutorial, we will discuss the following failure modes of language models, among others:

- **Low-quality low-probability words.** Due to their use of the softmax to compute $p_\theta(y_t \mid \mathbf{y}_{<t})$, language models place non-zero probability on poor continuations.
- **Degradation of long texts.** Possibly as a result of the above, generating longer texts can present a greater challenge, as errors tend to propagate and accumulate.
- **Repetition when searching for the mode.** In cases where *highly probable* text under the training set is desired, language models' probability estimates tend to fail and overestimate the probability of highly repetitive text.

High- and low-entropy generation. In some discussions around language generation, tasks are often discussed as "open-ended" (for example, story generation) or not (for example, machine translation). The techniques and histories of the corresponding literatures are often somewhat separate. We will discuss open-endedness as a scale well-described by the **entropy** of the true distribution a task specifies, as well as the entropy of the desired output behavior of the model. So, for example, in machine translation, the true distribution over correct translations has a relatively low entropy, even though texts (especially long ones) have a number of roughly equivalent translations; further, it is common to look for only the "most likely" translation. Story generation typically has more entropy (the set of nice stories is large) and the generation of arbitrary web text has more entropy still; further, the notion of the "most likely" web text document is unintuitive, to say the least. We will thus discuss models and the methods used to generate from them with the concept of entropy in mind, rather than using the more traditional (albeit qualitative) notion of open-endedness.

3.2 Part 2: Language Generation

Given a pretrained language model $p_\theta(\cdot \mid \mathbf{y}_{<t})$, how does ones generate text from it? There is a plethora of options available. We split these into two subgroups: deterministic and stochastic decoding strategies (Wiher et al., 2022).

Deterministic decoding. In tasks with one (or only a small number of) correct answers, researchers typically rely on deterministic strategies, which "search" over the support of the distribution $p_\theta(\cdot \mid \mathbf{y}_{<t})$ for this correct answer. In short, these strategies rely on some quantification of a string $\mathbf{y}$'s quality, e.g., its probability under p_θ, and they try to find the string which maximizes it. Finding this string, however, is an NP-hard problem (Chen et al., 2018). These decoding strategies thus propose heuristic methods for performing this search. Beam search, for instance, searches for this maximizing string by iteratively expanding all substrings $\mathbf{y}_{<t}$, albeit at any given point, keeping only the k best substrings found so far.

Stochastic decoding. In tasks for which text diversity is a desired attribute, stochastic strategies are usually employed. Typically, these strategies work incrementally: first, one word is sampled from $p_\theta(\cdot \mid \mathbf{y}_{<t})$; this word is then appended to the context, producing $\mathbf{y}_t$; the next word is then sampled from $p_\theta(\cdot \mid \mathbf{y}_{<t+1})$. Sampling stops at some pre-determined length, or once the end-of-string token is sampled. Following this iterative process, we sample strings according to distribution $p(\mathbf{y})$. Several issues arise from simply sampling from $p(\mathbf{y})$, though. In the next section, we dive into different methods to mitigate these issues.

3.3 Part 3: Sampling Adapters

As discussed in part 1, due to the structure of most probabilistic language generators, no token in the vocabulary can be assigned a probability of zero under $p_\theta(\cdot \mid \mathbf{y}_{<t})$. Even if a model assigns inappropriate tokens very low probability, there is still the chance of sampling them when using stochastic decoding strategies. This can lead to undesirable outputs, as a single incoherent token can render a natural language string virtually incomprehensible (Fan et al., 2018; Holtzman et al., 2020). While intuitively we might expect this issue to only occur with low probability, a concrete example proves otherwise. Let's say we have a model that assigns a very small collective probability mass of 0.1% to all tokens in the tail (low-probability region) of the distribution at any given point. If we sample a sequence of 200 tokens from this model, there is a $1-(1-0.001)^{200} \approx 20\%$ chance it will contain at least one token from the tail of the distribution.

In an attempt to prevent this issue, several works have proposed simple modifications to the sampling distribution to exclude undesirable tokens from the candidate pool. Two prominent examples are nucleus and top-k sampling, both of which truncate the distribution to some subset of its most probable items (and then renormalize it). These types of transformations are widely-employed when sampling from probabilistic language generators: they are quick to implement, efficient in practice, and surprisingly effective. Indeed, nucleus sampling is often used as a baseline in various language generation tasks (Welleck et al., 2020; Pillutla et al., 2021; Basu et al., 2021).

In this part of the tutorial, we will offer a formal treatment of these transformations; we present a general framework for what we call **sampling adapters**, the class of functions $g : \mathbb{R}^{|\mathcal{V}|} \rightarrow \mathbb{R}^{|\mathcal{V}|}$ that adapts each conditional distribution $p_\theta(\cdot \mid \mathbf{y}_{<t})$ in a locally normalized language model to a new distribution. We will discuss the motivation and formulation of several popular sampling adapters (Fan et al., 2018; Holtzman et al., 2020; Basu et al., 2021; Meister et al., 2022; Hewitt et al., 2022), describing the problems that they mitigate (such as sampling incoherent tokens) as well as the problems that they introduce (such as repetitive generations). Further, we will show results from prior works comparing these methods. Finally, we will discuss possible interpretations of the effectiveness of these methods, in order to provide intuition for why they lead to better language generation.

3.4 Part 4: Controlled Generation

Generated samples from language models often contain toxic or non-factual content (Gehman et al., 2020; Maynez et al., 2020). Further, they also often go off-topic, even after applying the sampling adapters discussed in the previous section (Yang and Klein, 2021). To ensure that the generated samples satisfy a set of desired properties—e.g. being non-toxic or talking about a certain topic—we need methods to impose controls during the sampling process. The question we will discuss in this part of the tutorial is how can we sample from a pretrained language model p_θ, while ensuring that samples satisfy a specific control c? This can be formalized as sampling from a conditional distribution $p_\theta(\mathbf{y} \mid c)$ instead. We split prior work on sampling from this distribution into two groups: autoregressive and non-autoregressive controlled generation methods.

Autoregressive generation. Similar to the decoding strategies discussed earlier, these methods incrementally generate text one token at a time, in a sequential manner. At each step of the generation, a token y_t is sampled with probability $p(y_t \mid \mathbf{y}_{<t}, c)$—which, following Bayes' rule, is proportional to $p_\theta(y_t \mid \mathbf{y}_{<t})\, p(c \mid \mathbf{y}_{\leq t})$ (Yang and Klein, 2021). In other words, at each timestep, the score of a candidate y_t under the language model $p_\theta(y_t \mid \mathbf{y}_{<t})$ is reweighted according to the probability that $\mathbf{y}_{\leq t}$ satisfies the control target: $p(c \mid \mathbf{y}_{\leq t})$. This control target is usually estimated with a supervised classifier parameterized by ϕ: $p_\phi(c \mid \mathbf{y}_{\leq t})$ (Ghazvininejad et al., 2017; Holtzman et al., 2018). The implication of this approach is that we need to have reliable estimates of how much a prefix satisfies the desired control. However, this is arguably an easier problem than building the entire distribution over natural language strings, if due to the smaller size of the support alone. Once we obtain such estimates, we can make use of an arbitrary language model p_θ for controlled generation.

Non-autoregressive generation. While autoregressive methods have proven effective for controlling the topic or the sentiment of samples, they fail for more complex controls such as toxicity or syntax. Particularly, for more complex controls, estimating $p(c \mid \mathbf{y}_{\leq t})$ becomes challenging. If at any point this probability distribution diverges from the true value, the error will propagate to the next steps due to structure of most of these models. To address this issue, non-autoregressive strategies propose to sample the whole sequence $\mathbf{y}$ at once. This is usually done by designing Markov-Chains based off of some (autoregressive) language model $p_\theta(\mathbf{y})$ that have the stationary distribution $p(\mathbf{y} \mid c)$. Given that the sampling space is high dimensional, Hamiltonian Monte Carlo (HMC) algorithms, such as Langevin Dynamics, have been shown to be effective for drawing samples from those Markov-Chains (Qin et al., 2022; Kumar et al., 2022).

3.5 Breadth of Research Covered

This tutorial is intended as a primer for recent language generation techniques. To this end, it will need to pull on research from a large number of authors, spanning several institutions. Explicitly, the background section on language modeling will cover, for example, works from OpenAI, Google, AI2, and DeepMind, as institutions with the resources to train these large language models and make them publicly available. The introduction to generation will touch on prominent methods, such as beam search (Graves, 2012), nucleus sampling (Holtzman et al., 2020), Mirostat (Basu et al., 2021), top-k sampling (Fan et al., 2018), typical decoding (Meister et al., 2022) and top-η sampling (Hewitt et al., 2022). The controlled generation section will summarize work on weighted decoding (Ghazvininejad et al., 2017; Holtzman et al., 2018), FUDGE (Yang and Klein, 2021), and recently proposed HMC-based methods (Qin et al., 2022; Kumar et al., 2022).

4 Presenters

- **Afra Amini** is a PhD student at ETH Zürich in the ETH AI Center. Her current foci include language generation and parsing.
- **Ryan Cotterell** is an assistant professor at ETH Zürich in the Institute for Machine Learning. His research focuses on a wide range of topics, including information-theoretic linguistics, parsing, computational typology and morphology, and bias and fairness in NLP systems.
- **John Hewitt** Is a PhD student at Stanford University. His research tackles basic problems in learning models from broad distributions over language, characterizing and understanding those models, and building smaller, simpler models.
- **Clara Meister** is a PhD student at ETH Zürich in the Institute for Machine Learning and a Google PhD Fellow. Her current foci include language generation, pyscholinguistics, and the general application of statistical methods to natural language processing.
- **Tiago Pimentel** is a PhD student at the University of Cambridge and a Facebook Fellow. His research focuses on information theory, and its applications to the analysis of pre-trained language models and natural languages.

Diversity Considerations

As our tutorial focuses on language generation, we will cover issues related to modeling and generating strings in languages which are typologically different from English. Further, this tutorial was developed by a group of researchers from three universities (Stanford, ETH and Cambridge), who are originally from 3 continents (Asia, North America, and South America). Lastly, it will discuss work produced by authors spanning many institutions and backgrounds (see § 3.5).

References

Sourya Basu, Govardana Sachitanandam Ramachandran, Nitish Shirish Keskar, and Lav R. Varshney. 2021. Mirostat: A perplexity-controlled neural text decoding algorithm. In *Proceedings of the 9th International Conference on Learning Representations.*

Yining Chen, Sorcha Gilroy, Andreas Maletti, Jonathan May, and Kevin Knight. 2018. Recurrent neural networks as weighted language recognizers. In *Proceedings of the 2018 Conference of the North American Chapter of the Association for Computational Linguistics: Human Language Technologies, Volume 1 (Long Papers)*, pages 2261–2271, New Orleans, Louisiana. Association for Computational Linguistics.

Angela Fan, Mike Lewis, and Yann Dauphin. 2018. Hierarchical neural story generation. In *Proceedings of the 56th Annual Meeting of the Association for Computational Linguistics (Volume 1: Long Papers)*, pages 889–898, Melbourne, Australia. Association for Computational Linguistics.

Samuel Gehman, Suchin Gururangan, Maarten Sap, Yejin Choi, and Noah A. Smith. 2020. RealToxicityPrompts: Evaluating neural toxic degeneration in language models. In *Findings of the Association for Computational Linguistics*, pages 3356–3369, Online. Association for Computational Linguistics.

Marjan Ghazvininejad, Xing Shi, Jay Priyadarshi, and Kevin Knight. 2017. Hafez: an interactive poetry generation system. In *Proceedings of ACL 2017, System Demonstrations*, pages 43–48, Vancouver, Canada. Association for Computational Linguistics.

Alex Graves. 2012. Sequence transduction with recurrent neural networks. *CoRR*, abs/1211.3711.

John Hewitt, Christopher D. Manning, and Percy Liang. 2022. Truncation sampling as language model desmoothing. In *Findings of the Conference on Empirical Methods in Natural Language Processing.*

Ari Holtzman, Jan Buys, Li Du, Maxwell Forbes, and Yejin Choi. 2020. The curious case of neural text degeneration. In *Proceedings of the 8th International Conference on Learning Representations.*

Ari Holtzman, Jan Buys, Maxwell Forbes, Antoine Bosselut, David Golub, and Yejin Choi. 2018. Learning to write with cooperative discriminators. In *Proceedings of the 56th Annual Meeting of the Association for Computational Linguistics (Volume 1: Long Papers)*, pages 1638–1649, Melbourne, Australia. Association for Computational Linguistics.

Sachin Kumar, Biswajit Paria, and Yulia Tsvetkov. 2022. Constrained sampling from language models via langevin dynamics in embedding spaces. *CoRR*, abs/2205.12558.

Joshua Maynez, Shashi Narayan, Bernd Bohnet, and Ryan McDonald. 2020. On faithfulness and factuality in abstractive summarization. In *Proceedings of the 58th Annual Meeting of the Association for Computational Linguistics*, pages 1906–1919, Online. Association for Computational Linguistics.

Clara Meister, Tiago Pimentel, Gian Wiher, and Ryan Cotterell. 2022. Locally typical sampling. *Transactions of the Association for Computational Linguistics.*

Krishna Pillutla, Swabha Swayamdipta, Rowan Zellers, John Thickstun, Sean Welleck, Yejin Choi, and Zaid Harchaoui. 2021. MAUVE: Measuring the gap between neural text and human text using divergence frontiers. In *Advances in Neural Information Processing Systems*, volume 34, pages 4816–4828. Curran Associates, Inc.

Lianhui Qin, Sean Welleck, Daniel Khashabi, and Yejin Choi. 2022. COLD decoding: Energy-based constrained text generation with langevin dynamics. In *Advances in Neural Information Processing Systems.*

Sean Welleck, Ilia Kulikov, Stephen Roller, Emily Dinan, Kyunghyun Cho, and Jason Weston. 2020. Neural text generation with unlikelihood training. In *Proceedings of the 8th International Conference on Learning Representations.*

Gian Wiher, Clara Meister, and Ryan Cotterell. 2022. On Decoding Strategies for Neural Text Generators. *Transactions of the Association for Computational Linguistics*, 10:997–1012.

Kevin Yang and Dan Klein. 2021. FUDGE: Controlled text generation with future discriminators. In *Proceedings of the 2021 Conference of the North American Chapter of the Association for Computational Linguistics: Human Language Technologies*, pages 3511–3535, Online. Association for Computational Linguistics.

Indirectly Supervised Natural Language Processing

Wenpeng Yin[†], Muhao Chen[‡], Ben Zhou[◇], Qiang Ning[⋆], Kai-Wei Chang[♯], Dan Roth[◇⋆]
[†]Penn State; [‡]USC; [◇]UPenn; [⋆]AWS AI Labs; [♯]UCLA
wenpeng@psu.edu; muhaoche@usc.edu
{xyzhou,danroth}@seas.upenn.edu
qning@amazon.com; kwchang@cs.ucla.edu

Abstract

This tutorial targets researchers and practitioners who are interested in ML technologies for NLP from indirect supervision. In particular, we will present a diverse thread of indirect supervision studies that try to answer the following questions: (i) when and how can we provide supervision for a target task T, if all we have is data that corresponds to a "related" task T'? (ii) humans do not use *exhaustive* supervision; they rely on occasional feedback, and learn from incidental signals from various sources; how can we effectively incorporate such supervision in machine learning? (iii) how can we leverage multi-modal supervision to help NLP? To the end, we will discuss several lines of research that address those challenges, including (i) indirect supervision from T' that handles T with outputs spanning from a moderate size to an open space, (ii) the use of sparsely occurring and incidental signals, such as partial labels, noisy labels, knowledge-based constraints, and cross-domain or cross-task annotations—all having statistical associations with the task, (iii) principled ways to measure and understand why these incidental signals can contribute to our target tasks, and (iv) indirect supervision from vision-language signals. We will conclude the tutorial by outlining directions for further investigation.

1 Introduction

Conventional approaches to NLP rely on task-specific labeled examples of a large volume. This does not apply to scenarios where tasks may be too complicated or costly to annotate, or the system is required to handle a new task immediately. Many people increasingly perceive that pretrained language models (PLMs) use self-supervision, and therefore there is no need for supervision anymore. While this is probably true for Encoder-only models (e.g., BERT (Devlin et al., 2019)), this does not hold for Decoder models, where people nowadays use vast amounts of supervision and reinforcement learning signals. Therefore, it is still desirable to gather *supervision that has already existed in related tasks or is pretty cheap*, which is termed "indirect supervision" in this tutorial.

Recently, there have been increasing works that study indirect supervision for a wide range of NLP tasks. For example, Yin et al. (2019) and Lu et al. (2022a) respectively leveraged the rich annotation of a source task (natural language inference or summarization) to address the poorly-annotated target tasks. To make better use of the natural texts, some literature (Roth, 2017; Chen et al., 2021; He et al., 2021) proposed to explore incidental supervision, e.g., phonetic similarity and similar temporal distribution for named entity transliteration, to help downstream tasks. That sort of incidental supervision is often weak signals that exist in the data and the environment independently of the tasks at hand, and is hard to be encoded by PLMs. Furthermore, when accessing supervision from pure text is challenging, researchers turned to other modalities for indirect supervision (Li et al., 2022b).

This tutorial presents a comprehensive introduction of those lines of frontier research on indirectly supervised NLP. In particular, it tries to answer the following questions: (i) Which source task is easier to be adapted to solve various target tasks and any constraints there? (ii) What are the limitations of pretrained language models in discovering supervision from natural texts, and how can we alleviate them with incidental signals? (iii) Are there any theoretical measures that can indicate the benefits of the incidental signals to a given downstream task? (iv) How to mitigate the gap between different modalities if we want to utilize image/video knowledge to guide NLP? By addressing those critical questions, we believe it is necessary to present a timely tutorial to comprehensively summarize the new frontiers in indirectly supervised NLP research and point out the emerging challenges that deserve further investigation. Participants will learn about

Proceedings of the 61st Annual Meeting of the Association for Computational Linguistics
Volume 6: Tutorial Abstracts, pages 32–40
July 9, 2023

recent trends and emerging challenges in this topic, representative tools and learning resources to obtain ready-to-use models, and how related technologies benefit end-user NLP applications.

2 Outline of Tutorial Content

This **half-day** tutorial presents a systematic overview of recent advancements in indirect supervision methods for NLP. The detailed contents are outlined below.

2.1 Background and Motivation [15min]

We will begin motivating this topic with a selection of real-world applications and emerging challenges of NLP with limited end-task annotations.

2.2 Indirect Supervision from NLU Tasks [30min]

We start with indirect supervision from a source task that is efficient to handle a moderate size of outputs in the target task. For example, in most zero/few-shot text classification tasks, such as topic classification, entity typing, relation identification, etc., the main obstacle is letting systems understand the semantics of labels. In contrast to conventional supervised classifiers, which converted labels into indices, we introduce NLI (natural language inference)-based approaches that take into account the input semantics as well as label semantics. In specific, we will introduce typical work that treats different topics (Yin et al., 2019), stances (Xu et al., 2022), entity types (Li et al., 2022a; Du et al., 2023), event types (Lyu et al., 2021), entity relations (Xia et al., 2021; Sainz et al., 2021, 2022), and question-answer (Yin et al., 2021) as hypotheses and the inputs as premises, then makes use of pretrained NLI system to handle a variety of classification tasks with a given set of labels.

In addition, we will present extractive question answering (Ex-QA) based supervision that is utilized for downstream tasks (McCann et al., 2018; Keskar et al., 2019; He et al., 2020; Wu et al., 2020; Li et al., 2020). The advantage of Ex-QA based indirect supervision over the NLI-based one lies in that Ex-QA can handle sequence tagging and span detection tasks while NLI-based approaches primarily work for classification.

2.3 Indirect Supervision from NLG and IR [30min]

We will introduce methodologies that acquire indirect supervision signals from natural language generation (NLG) and information retrieval tasks to solve more low-resource discriminative tasks. Formulating discriminative tasks as generation tasks can be an efficient way to guide PLMs to leverage the semantics of decision labels (Huang et al., 2021; Lu et al., 2022a; Hsu et al., 2022; Yuan et al., 2022). A method of this kind typically leads to a sequence-to-sequence generation process that emits a verbalization of the decision label given the input sequence (Zeng et al., 2018, 2020; Ye et al., 2021; Cao and Ananiadou, 2021). Instead of predicting classification logits, these models represent the class as a concise structure and employ controlled decoding for the generation. In this way, the model allows cross-task signal transfer from high-resource NLG tasks, and captures a semantically rich representation of the discriminative task's original decision space. A representative example is SuRE (Lu et al., 2022a), which reformulates the more expensive relation extraction task into summarization with constrained decoding, leading to more precise and label-efficient sentence-level relation extraction. We will also introduce methods that reformulate as a retrieval task (Zhang et al., 2021a,b; Huang et al., 2022; Chen et al., 2020). This technique allows using the inductive bias of a dense retrieval model to handle a discriminative task with a large decision space, such as entity linking (Zhang et al., 2021a) and fine-grained typing (Huang et al., 2022).

2.4 Incidental Supervision from Natural Text [30min]

Both the indirect supervision introduced in the above sections (§2.2-§2.3) relies on transferred supervision signals from some source task annotations. Natural texts are structured to contain a large number of incidental signals that can be subsequently utilized by downstream tasks with minimal human effort. Despite the fact that the community has found that PLMs are capable of providing incidental supervision signals for a wide range of tasks, they do not provide controls over what kinds of knowledge exist. To the end, we introduce incidental relations found in natural text spans. For example, certain keywords and linguistic patterns can provide incidental supervision to downstream tasks such as relation extraction (Zhou et al., 2022b), temporal reasoning (Zhou et al., 2020, 2021), and affordance reasoning (Qasemi et al., 2022). Moreover, textual snippets can often be viewed in a structure by their global information, such as publication dates, titles, and authors, which establish relations that helps with complex tasks (Zhou et al., 2022a). Designing and collecting such linguistic patterns often require human knowledge; this process of injecting human knowledge provides signals that PLMs cannot find and produces diverse automatic supervision for many tasks.

2.5 Theoretical Analysis of Incidental Supervision [30min]

§2.4 presents several real-world applications of incidental signals. In this part, we pose the challenge to define a principled way to measure the benefits of these signals to a given downstream task, and the challenge to further understand why and how these signals can help reduce the complexity of the learning problem in theory. We will introduce existing efforts along these two lines, mainly He et al. (2021) and Wang et al. (2020). Specifically, we introduce (i) a unified theoretical framework (Wang et al., 2020) for multi-class classification when the supervision is provided by a variable that contains nonzero mutual information with the gold label; the nature of this problem is determined by the transition probability from the gold labels to the indirect supervision variables (van Rooyen and Williamson, 2018) and the learner's prior knowledge about the transition; and (ii) a unified PAC-Bayesian motivated informativeness measure, PABI (He et al., 2021), that characterizes the uncertainty reduction provided by incidental supervision signals. We share studies in Qasemi et al. (2022) and Ning et al. (2019) that demonstrate PABI's effectiveness by quantifying the value added by various types of incidental signals to sequence tagging tasks. Finally, we will highlight the gaps that are yet to be closed in these lines, and point out future research directions on this topic.

2.6 Indirect Supervision from Multi-modalities [30min]

In the previous section, we discuss how to leverage indirect supervision from text data. Next, we will extend our discussion to introduce methods that leverage indirect supervision in multimodal data for cross-modality tasks. We will take vision-language tasks, such as answering complex high-level question about images (Zellers et al., 2019), as an example. We will first introduce methods that learn to align visual tokens and text tokens based on image caption data (Tan and Bansal, 2019; Li et al., 2019; Tan and Bansal, 2020). The cross-modality knowledge learned from indirect supervision can be used to solve various text, image, and mixed modality tasks. We will then introduce approaches that use only indirect supervision from object recognition models to learn text-image alignment from unaligned language and vision Data (Li et al., 2021). Finally, we will discuss methods for learning to ground elements of language to image regions without explicit supervision (Li et al., 2022b; Zhang et al., 2022).

2.7 Future Research Directions [15min]

Indirect supervision is the key to coping with a variety of NLP tasks that are not equipped with enough labeled data. We will conclude the tutorial by presenting further challenges and potential research topics, such as (i) explaining the model predictions when the supervision is indirect (Rajani et al., 2020; Lu et al., 2022b), (ii) injecting incidental signals that express human knowledge but cannot be learned by pretrained language models from natural texts (Yu et al., 2022), and (iii) task instructions as supervision (Wang et al., 2022).

3 Specification of the Tutorial

The proposed tutorial is considered a **cutting-edge** tutorial that introduces new frontiers in indirectly supervised NLP. The presented topic has not been covered by any *CL tutorials in the past 4 years.

Audience and Prerequisites Based on the level of interest in this topic, we expect around 150 participants. While no specific background knowledge is assumed of the audience, it would be best for the attendees to know about basic deep learning technologies, pre-trained language models (e.g. BERT). A reading list that could help provide background knowledge to the audience before attending this tutorial is given in Appx. §A.2.

Breadth We estimate that at least 60% of the work covered in this tutorial is from researchers other than the instructors of the tutorial.

Diversity Considerations This tutorial will cover indirect supervision from beyond text. We will also cover content around how indirect supervision can be applicable to a variety of low-resourced tasks. Our presenter team has a diverse background from both academia (including assistant, associate, distinguished professors, and a senior Ph.D. student) and industry (a senior scientist at AWS AI).

Our instructor team will promote our tutorial on social media to diversify our audience participation.

Material Access Online Open Access All the materials are openly available at `https://cogcomp.seas.upenn.edu/page/tutorial.202307`

4 Tutorial Instructors

The following are biographies of the speakers. Past tutorials given by us are listed in Appx. §A.1.

Wenpeng Yin is an Assistant Professor in the Department of Computer Science and Engineering at Penn State University. Prior to joining Penn State, he was a tenure-track faculty member at Temple University (1/2022-12/2022), Senior Research Scientist at Salesforce Research (8/2019-12/2021), a postdoctoral researcher at UPenn (10/2017-7/2019), and got his Ph.D. degree from the Ludwig Maximilian University of Munich, Germany, in 2017. Dr. Yin's research focuses on natural language processing with three sub-areas: (i) learning from task instructions; (ii) information extraction; (iii) learning with limited supervision. Additional information is available at `www.wenpengyin.org`.

Muhao Chen is an Assistant Research Professor of Computer Science at USC, where he directs the Language Understanding and Knowledge Acquisition (LUKA) Group. His research focuses on data-driven machine learning approaches for natural language understanding and knowledge acquisition. His work has been recognized with an NSF CRII Award, a Cisco Faculty Research Award, an ACM SIGBio Best Student Paper Award, and a Best Paper Nomination at CoNLL. Muhao obtained his PhD degree from UCLA Department of Computer Science in 2019, and was a postdoctoral researcher at UPenn prior to joining USC. Additional information is available at `http://luka-group.github.io`.

Ben Zhou is a fourth-year Ph.D. student at the Department of Computer and Information Science, University of Pennsylvania. Ben's research interests are distant supervision extraction and experiential knowledge reasoning, and he has more than 5 recent papers on related topics. He is a recipient of the ENIAC fellowship from the University of Pennsylvania, and a finalist of the CRA outstanding undergraduate researcher award. Additional information is available at `http://xuanyu.me/`.

Qiang Ning is currently a senior applied scientist at AWS AI (2022-). Prior to that, Qiang was an applied scientist at Alexa AI (2020-2022) and a research scientist at the Allen Institute for AI (2019-2020). Qiang received his Ph.D. from the University of Illinois at Urbana-Champaign in 2019 in Electrical and Computer Engineering. Qiang's research interests span in information extraction, question answering, and the application of weak supervision methods in these NLP problems in both theoretical and practical aspects. Additional information is available at `https://www.qiangning.info/`.

Kai-Wei Chang is an associate professor in the Department of Computer Science at the University of California Los Angeles. His research interests include designing robust, fair, and accountable machine learning methods for building reliable NLP systems. His awards include the EMNLP Best Long Paper Award (2017), the KDD Best Paper Award (2010), and the Sloan Resaerch Fellowship (2021). Kai-Wei has given tutorials at NAACL 15, AAAI 16, FAccT18, EMNLP 19, AAAI 20, EMNLP 21, MLSS 21 on different research topics. Additional information is available at `http://kwchang.net`.

Dan Roth is the Eduardo D. Glandt Distinguished Professor at the Department of Computer and Information Science, UPenn, the NLP Lead at AWS AI Labs, and a Fellow of the AAAS, ACM, AAAI, and ACL. In 2017 Roth was awarded the John McCarthy Award, the highest award the AI community gives to mid-career AI researchers. Roth was recognized "for major conceptual and theoretical advances in the modeling of natural language understanding, machine learning, and reasoning." Roth has published broadly in machine learning, NLP, KRR, and learning theory, and has given keynote talks and tutorials in all ACL and AAAI major conferences. Roth was the Editor-in-Chief of JAIR until 2017, and was the program chair of AAAI'11, ACL'03 and CoNLL'02; he serves regularly as an area chair and senior program committee member in the major conferences in his research areas. Additional information is available at `www.cis.upenn.edu/~danroth`.

Acknowledgement

This presenters' research is supported in part by Contract FA8750-19-2-1004 with the US Defense Advanced Research Projects Agency (DARPA), the DARPA MCS program under Contract No. N66001-19-2-4033 with the United States Office Of Naval Research, Intelligence Advanced Research Projects Activity (IARPA) Contract No. 2019-19051600006 under the BETTER Program, the National Science Foundation (NSF) of United States Grant IIS 2105329, a subaward from NSF Cloudbank 1925001 through UCSD, an Amazon Research Award and a Cisco Research Award. The views and conclusions contained herein are those of the authors and should not be interpreted as necessarily representing the official policies, either expressed or implied, of DARPA, or the U.S. Government. The U.S. Government is authorized to reproduce and distribute reprints for governmental purposes notwithstanding any copyright annotation therein,

Ethical Considerations

We do not anticipate any ethical issues particularly to the topics of the tutorial. Nevertheless, some work presented in this tutorial extensively uses large-scale pretrained models with self-attention, which may lead to substantial financial and environmental costs.

References

Jiarun Cao and Sophia Ananiadou. 2021. GenerativeRE: Incorporating a novel copy mechanism and pretrained model for joint entity and relation extraction. In *Findings of the Association for Computational Linguistics: EMNLP 2021*, pages 2119–2126, Punta Cana, Dominican Republic. Association for Computational Linguistics.

Muhao Chen, Weijia Shi, Ben Zhou, and Dan Roth. 2021. Cross-lingual entity alignment with incidental supervision. In *Proceedings of the 16th Conference of the European Chapter of the Association for Computational Linguistics: Main Volume, EACL 2021, Online, April 19 - 23, 2021*, pages 645–658. Association for Computational Linguistics.

Muhao Chen, Hongming Zhang, Haoyu Wang, and Dan Roth. 2020. What are you trying to do? semantic typing of event processes. In *Proceedings of the 24th Conference on Computational Natural Language Learning*, pages 531–542, Online. Association for Computational Linguistics.

Jacob Devlin, Ming-Wei Chang, Kenton Lee, and Kristina Toutanova. 2019. BERT: pre-training of deep bidirectional transformers for language understanding. In *Proceedings of the 2019 Conference of the North American Chapter of the Association for Computational Linguistics: Human Language Technologies, NAACL-HLT 2019, Minneapolis, MN, USA, June 2-7, 2019, Volume 1 (Long and Short Papers)*, pages 4171–4186.

Jiangshu Du, Wenpeng Yin, Congying Xia, and Philip S. Yu. 2023. Learning to select from multiple options. In *AAAI*.

Hangfeng He, Qiang Ning, and Dan Roth. 2020. Quase: Question-answer driven sentence encoding. In *Proceedings of the 58th Annual Meeting of the Association for Computational Linguistics, ACL 2020, Online, July 5-10, 2020*, pages 8743–8758.

Hangfeng He, Mingyuan Zhang, Qiang Ning, and Dan Roth. 2021. Foreseeing the Benefits of Incidental Supervision. In *Proc. of the Conference on Empirical Methods in Natural Language Processing (EMNLP)*.

I-Hung Hsu, Kuan-Hao Huang, Elizabeth Boschee, Scott Miller, Prem Natarajan, Kai-Wei Chang, and Nanyun Peng. 2022. DEGREE: A data-efficient generation-based event extraction model. In *Proceedings of the 2022 Conference of the North American Chapter of the Association for Computational Linguistics: Human Language Technologies*, pages 1890–1908, Seattle, United States. Association for Computational Linguistics.

James Y. Huang, Bangzheng Li, Jiashu Xu, and Muhao Chen. 2022. Unified semantic typing with meaningful label inference. In *Proceedings of the 2022 Conference of the North American Chapter of the Association for Computational Linguistics: Human Language Technologies*, pages 2642–2654, Seattle, United States. Association for Computational Linguistics.

Kung-Hsiang Huang, Sam Tang, and Nanyun Peng. 2021. Document-level entity-based extraction as template generation. In *Proceedings of the 2021 Conference on Empirical Methods in Natural Language Processing*, pages 5257–5269, Online and Punta Cana, Dominican Republic. Association for Computational Linguistics.

Nitish Shirish Keskar, Bryan McCann, Caiming Xiong, and Richard Socher. 2019. Unifying question answering and text classification via span extraction. *CoRR*, abs/1904.09286.

Bangzheng Li, Wenpeng Yin, and Muhao Chen. 2022a. Ultra-fine entity typing with indirect supervision from natural language inference. *Transactions of the Association for Computational Linguistics*, 10:607–622.

Liunian Harold Li, Mark Yatskar, Da Yin, Cho-Jui Hsieh, and Kai-Wei Chang. 2019. Visualbert: A simple and performant baseline for vision and language. In *Arxiv*.

Liunian Harold Li, Haoxuan You, Zhecan Wang, Alireza Zareian, Shih-Fu Chang, and Kai-Wei Chang. 2021. Unsupervised vision-and-language pre-training without parallel images and captions. In *Proceedings of the 2021 Conference of the North American Chapter of the Association for Computational Linguistics: Human Language Technologies*, pages 5339–5350, Online. Association for Computational Linguistics.

Liunian Harold Li, Pengchuan Zhang, Haotian Zhang, Jianwei Yang, Chunyuan Li, Yiwu Zhong, Lijuan Wang, Lu Yuan, Lei Zhang, Jenq-Neng Hwang, Kai-Wei Chang, and Jianfeng Gao. 2022b. Grounded language-image pre-training. In *IEEE/CVF Conference on Computer Vision and Pattern Recognition, CVPR 2022, New Orleans, LA, USA, June 18-24, 2022*, pages 10955–10965. IEEE.

Xiaoya Li, Jingrong Feng, Yuxian Meng, Qinghong Han, Fei Wu, and Jiwei Li. 2020. A unified MRC framework for named entity recognition. In *Proceedings of the 58th Annual Meeting of the Association for Computational Linguistics*, pages 5849–5859, Online. Association for Computational Linguistics.

Keming Lu, I-Hung Hsu, Mingyu Derek Ma, Wenxuan Zhou, and Muhao Chen. 2022a. Summarization as indirect supervision for relation extraction. In *EMNLP - Findings*.

Pan Lu, Swaroop Mishra, Tony Xia, Liang Qiu, Kai-Wei Chang, Song-Chun Zhu, Oyvind Tafjord, Peter Clark, and Ashwin Kalyan. 2022b. Learn to explain: Multimodal reasoning via thought chains for science question answering. In *NeurIPS*.

Qing Lyu, Hongming Zhang, Elior Sulem, and Dan Roth. 2021. Zero-shot event extraction via transfer learning: Challenges and insights. In *Proceedings of the 59th Annual Meeting of the Association for Computational Linguistics and the 11th International Joint Conference on Natural Language Processing (Volume 2: Short Papers)*, pages 322–332, Online. Association for Computational Linguistics.

Bryan McCann, Nitish Shirish Keskar, Caiming Xiong, and Richard Socher. 2018. The natural language decathlon: Multitask learning as question answering. *CoRR*, abs/1806.08730.

Qiang Ning, Hangfeng He, Chuchu Fan, and Dan Roth. 2019. Partial or Complete, That's The Question. In *Proc. of the Annual Conference of the North American Chapter of the Association for Computational Linguistics (NAACL)*.

Ehsan Qasemi, Piyush Khanna, Qiang Ning, and Muhao Chen. 2022. PInKS: Preconditioned commonsense inference with minimal supervision. In *Proceedings of the 2nd Conference of the Asia-Pacific Chapter of the Association for Computational Linguistics and the 12th International Joint Conference on Natural Language Processing (Volume 1: Long Papers)*, pages 320–336, Online only. Association for Computational Linguistics.

Nazneen Fatema Rajani, Ben Krause, Wengpeng Yin, Tong Niu, Richard Socher, and Caiming Xiong. 2020. Explaining and improving model behavior with k nearest neighbor representations. *CoRR*, abs/2010.09030.

Dan Roth. 2017. Incidental supervision: Moving beyond supervised learning. In *Proceedings of the Thirty-First AAAI Conference on Artificial Intelligence, February 4-9, 2017, San Francisco, California, USA*, pages 4885–4890.

Oscar Sainz, Oier Lopez de Lacalle, Gorka Labaka, Ander Barrena, and Eneko Agirre. 2021. Label verbalization and entailment for effective zero and few-shot relation extraction. In *Proceedings of the 2021 Conference on Empirical Methods in Natural Language Processing, EMNLP 2021, Virtual Event / Punta Cana, Dominican Republic, 7-11 November, 2021*, pages 1199–1212.

Oscar Sainz, Itziar Gonzalez-Dios, Oier Lopez de Lacalle, Bonan Min, and Eneko Agirre. 2022. Textual entailment for event argument extraction: Zero- and few-shot with multi-source learning. In *Findings of the Association for Computational Linguistics: NAACL 2022, Seattle, WA, United States, July 10-15, 2022*, pages 2439–2455.

Hao Tan and Mohit Bansal. 2019. LXMERT: Learning cross-modality encoder representations from transformers. In *Proceedings of the 2019 Conference on Empirical Methods in Natural Language Processing and the 9th International Joint Conference on Natural Language Processing (EMNLP-IJCNLP)*, pages 5100–5111, Hong Kong, China. Association for Computational Linguistics.

Hao Tan and Mohit Bansal. 2020. Vokenization: Improving language understanding with contextualized, visual-grounded supervision. In *Proceedings of the 2020 Conference on Empirical Methods in Natural Language Processing (EMNLP)*, pages 2066–2080, Online. Association for Computational Linguistics.

Brendan van Rooyen and Robert C. Williamson. 2018. A Theory of Learning with Corrupted Labels. *Journal of Machine Learning Research*, 18(228):1–50.

Kaifu Wang, Qiang Ning, and Dan Roth. 2020. Learnability with Indirect Supervision Signals. In *Proc. of the Conference on Neural Information Processing Systems (NeurIPS)*.

Yizhong Wang, Swaroop Mishra, Pegah Alipoormolabashi, Yeganeh Kordi, Amirreza Mirzaei, Anjana Arunkumar, Arjun Ashok, Arut Selvan Dhanasekaran, Atharva Naik, David Stap, Eshaan Pathak, Giannis Karamanolakis, Haizhi Gary Lai, Ishan Purohit, Ishani Mondal, Jacob Anderson, Kirby Kuznia, Krima Doshi, Maitreya Patel, Kuntal Kumar Pal, Mehrad Moradshahi, Mihir Parmar, Mirali Purohit, Neeraj Varshney, Phani Rohitha Kaza, Pulkit Verma, Ravsehaj Singh Puri, Rushang Karia, Shailaja Keyur Sampat, Savan Doshi, Siddhartha

Mishra, Sujan Reddy, Sumanta Patro, Tanay Dixit, Xudong Shen, Chitta Baral, Yejin Choi, Hannaneh Hajishirzi, Noah A. Smith, and Daniel Khashabi. 2022. Benchmarking generalization via in-context instructions on 1, 600+ language tasks. *CoRR*, abs/2204.07705.

Wei Wu, Fei Wang, Arianna Yuan, Fei Wu, and Jiwei Li. 2020. CorefQA: Coreference resolution as query-based span prediction. In *Proceedings of the 58th Annual Meeting of the Association for Computational Linguistics*, pages 6953–6963, Online. Association for Computational Linguistics.

Congying Xia, Wenpeng Yin, Yihao Feng, and Philip S. Yu. 2021. Incremental few-shot text classification with multi-round new classes: Formulation, dataset and system. In *Proceedings of the 2021 Conference of the North American Chapter of the Association for Computational Linguistics: Human Language Technologies, NAACL-HLT 2021, Online, June 6-11, 2021*, pages 1351–1360.

Hanzi Xu, Slobodan Vucetic, and Wenpeng Yin. 2022. Openstance: Real-world zero-shot stance detection. volume Proceedings of CoNLL.

Hongbin Ye, Ningyu Zhang, Shumin Deng, Mosha Chen, Chuanqi Tan, Fei Huang, and Huajun Chen. 2021. Contrastive triple extraction with generative transformer. In *AAAI*.

Wenpeng Yin, Jamaal Hay, and Dan Roth. 2019. Benchmarking zero-shot text classification: Datasets, evaluation and entailment approach. In *Proceedings of the 2019 Conference on Empirical Methods in Natural Language Processing and the 9th International Joint Conference on Natural Language Processing, EMNLP-IJCNLP 2019, Hong Kong, China, November 3-7, 2019*, pages 3912–3921.

Wenpeng Yin, Dragomir R. Radev, and Caiming Xiong. 2021. Docnli: A large-scale dataset for document-level natural language inference. In *Findings of ACL/IJCNLP*, pages 4913–4922.

Donghan Yu, Chenguang Zhu, Yiming Yang, and Michael Zeng. 2022. Jaket: Joint pre-training of knowledge graph and language understanding. In *Proceedings of the AAAI Conference on Artificial Intelligence*, volume 36, pages 11630–11638.

Hongyi Yuan, Zheng Yuan, and Sheng Yu. 2022. Generative biomedical entity linking via knowledge base-guided pre-training and synonyms-aware fine-tuning. In *Proceedings of the 2022 Conference of the North American Chapter of the Association for Computational Linguistics: Human Language Technologies*, pages 4038–4048, Seattle, United States. Association for Computational Linguistics.

Rowan Zellers, Yonatan Bisk, Ali Farhadi, and Yejin Choi. 2019. From recognition to cognition: Visual commonsense reasoning. In *The IEEE Conference on Computer Vision and Pattern Recognition (CVPR)*.

Daojian Zeng, Haoran Zhang, and Qianying Liu. 2020. Copymtl: Copy mechanism for joint extraction of entities and relations with multi-task learning. In *Proceedings of the AAAI conference on artificial intelligence*, volume 34, pages 9507–9514.

Xiangrong Zeng, Daojian Zeng, Shizhu He, Kang Liu, and Jun Zhao. 2018. Extracting relational facts by an end-to-end neural model with copy mechanism. In *Proceedings of the 56th Annual Meeting of the Association for Computational Linguistics (Volume 1: Long Papers)*, pages 506–514, Melbourne, Australia. Association for Computational Linguistics.

Haotian* Zhang, Pengchuan* Zhang, Xiaowei Hu, Yen-Chun Chen, Liunian Harold Li, Xiyang Dai, Lijuan Wang, Lu Yuan, Jenq-Neng Hwang, and Jianfeng Gao. 2022. Glipv2: Unifying localization and vision-language understanding. *arXiv preprint arXiv:2206.05836*.

Wenzheng Zhang, Wenyue Hua, and Karl Stratos. 2021a. Entqa: Entity linking as question answering. In *International Conference on Learning Representations*.

Yue Zhang, Hongliang Fei, and Ping Li. 2021b. Readsre: Retrieval-augmented distantly supervised relation extraction. In *Proceedings of the 44th International ACM SIGIR Conference on Research and Development in Information Retrieval*, pages 2257–2262.

Ben Zhou, Qiang Ning, Daniel Khashabi, and Dan Roth. 2020. Temporal Common Sense Acquisition with Minimal Supervision. In *Proc. of the Annual Meeting of the Association for Computational Linguistics (ACL)*.

Ben Zhou, Kyle Richardson, Qiang Ning, Tushar Khot, Ashish Sabharwal, and Dan Roth. 2021. Temporal reasoning on implicit events from distant supervision. *NAACL*.

Ben Zhou, Kyle Richardson, Xiaodong Yu, and Dan Roth. 2022a. Learning to decompose: Hypothetical question decomposition based on comparable texts. *EMNLP*.

Ben Zhou, Dian Yu, Dong Yu, and Dan Roth. 2022b. Cross-lingual speaker identification using distant supervision. *Arxiv*.

A Appendix

A.1 Past Tutorials by the Instructors

The presenters of this tutorial have given the following tutorials at leading international conferences in the past.

- Muhao Chen:
  - NAACL'22: New Frontiers of Information Extraction.

- ACL'21: Event-Centric Natural Language Processing.
- AAAI'21: Event-Centric Natural Language Understanding.
- KDD'21: From Tables to Knowledge: Recent Advances in Table Understanding.
- AAAI'20: Recent Advances of Transferable Representation Learning.

• Qiang Ning:

- ACL'21: Event-Centric Natural Language Processing.
- AAAI'21: Event-Centric Natural Language Understanding.

• Ben Zhou:

- NAACL'22: New Frontiers of Information Extraction

• Kai-Wei Chang:

- EMNLP'21: Robustness and Adversarial Examples in Natural Language Processing
- AAAI'20: Recent Advances of Transferable Representation Learning.
- EMNLP '19: A tutorial on Bias and Fairness in Natural Language Processing.
- ACM FAT*'18: A tutorial on Quantifying and Reducing Gender Stereotypes in Word Embeddings.
- TAAI'17: A tutorial on Structured Predictions: Practical Advancements and Applications in Natural Language Processing.
- AAAI'16: A tutorial on Learning and Inference in Structured Prediction Models.
- NAACL'15: A tutorial on Hands-on Learning to Search for Structured Prediction.

• Dan Roth:

- NAACL'22: New Frontiers of Information Extraction.
- ACL'21: Event-Centric Natural Language Processing.
- AAAI'21: Event-Centric Natural Language Understanding.
- ACL'20: Commonsense Reasoning for Natural Language Processing.
- AAAI'20: Recent Advances of Transferable Representation Learning.
- ACL'18: A tutorial on Multi-lingual Entity Discovery and Linking.
- EACL'17: A tutorial on Integer Linear Programming Formulations in Natural Language Processing.
- AAAI'16: A tutorial on Structured Prediction.
- ACL'14: A tutorial on Wikification and Entity Linking.
- AAAI'13: Information Trustworthiness.
- COLING'12: A Tutorial on Temporal Information Extraction and Shallow Temporal Reasoning.
- NAACL'12: A Tutorial on Constrained Conditional Models: Structured Predictions in NLP.
- NAACL'10: A Tutorial on Integer Linear Programming Methods in NLP.
- EACL'09: A Tutorial on Constrained Conditional Models.
- ACL'07: A Tutorial on Textual Entailment.

A.2 Recommended Paper List

The following is a reading list that could help provide background knowledge to the audience before attending this tutorial:

• Wenpeng Yin, Jamaal Hay, Dan Roth. Benchmarking Zero-shot Text Classification: Datasets, Evaluation and Entailment Approach. EMNLP 2019.

• Oscar Sainz, Itziar Gonzalez-Dios, Oier Lopez de Lacalle, Bonan Min, Eneko Agirre. Textual Entailment for Event Argument Extraction: Zero- and Few-Shot with Multi-Source Learning. Findings of NAACL 2022.

• Wenzheng Zhang, Wenyue Hua, Karl Stratos. EntQA: Entity Linking as Question Answering. ICLR 2022.

• Keming Lu, I-Hung Hsu, Wenxuan Zhou, Mingyu Derek Ma, Muhao Chen. Summarization as Indirect Supervision for Relation Extraction. EMNLP - Findings, 2022.

• Sarah Wiegreffe, Jack Hessel, Swabha Swayamdipta, Mark O. Riedl, Yejin Choi. Reframing human-AI collaboration for generating free-text explanations. NAACL, 2022.

• Ben Zhou, Kyle Richardson, Xiaodong Yu, Dan Roth. Learning to decompose: Hypothetical question decomposition based on comparable texts. EMNLP, 2022.

• Hangfeng He, Mingyuan Zhang, Qiang Ning, and Dan Roth. Foreseeing the Benefits of Incidental Supervision. EMNLP 2021.

• Kaifu Wang, Qiang Ning, and Dan Roth. Learnability with Indirect Supervision Signals. NeurIPS 2020.

- Rowan Zellers, Yonatan Bisk, Ali Farhadi, and Yejin Choi. From recognition to cognition: Visual commonsense reasoning. CVPR 2019.
- Hao Tan and Mohit Bansal. Vokenization: Improving language understanding with contextualized, visual-grounded supervision. EMNLP 2020.

Tutorial Proposal: Retrieval-based Language Models and Applications

Akari Asai[†] **Sewon Min**[†] **Zexuan Zhong**[‡] **Danqi Chen**[‡]
[†] University of Washington [‡]Princeton University
{akari,sewon}@cs.washington.edu
{zzhong,danqic}@cs.princeton.edu

1 Description

Language models (LMs) such as GPT-3 (Brown et al., 2020) and PaLM (Chowdhery et al., 2022) have shown impressive abilities in a range of natural language processing (NLP) tasks. However, relying solely on their parameters to encode a wealth of world knowledge requires a prohibitively large number of parameters and hence massive compute, and they often struggle to learn long-rail knowledge (Roberts et al., 2020; Kandpal et al., 2022; Mallen et al., 2022). Moreover, these parametric LMs are fundamentally incapable of adapting over time (De Cao et al., 2021; Lazaridou et al., 2021; Kasai et al., 2022), often hallucinate (Shuster et al., 2021), and may leak private data from the training corpus (Carlini et al., 2021). To overcome these limitations, there has been growing interest in retrieval-based LMs (Guu et al., 2020; Khandelwal et al., 2020; Borgeaud et al., 2022; Zhong et al., 2022; Izacard et al., 2022b; Min et al., 2022), which incorporate a non-parametric datastore (e.g., text chunks from an external corpus) with their parametric counterparts. Retrieval-based LMs can outperform LMs without retrieval by a large margin with much fewer parameters (Mallen et al., 2022), can update their knowledge by replacing their retrieval corpora (Izacard et al., 2022b), and provide citations for users to easily verify and evaluate the predictions (Menick et al., 2022; Bohnet et al., 2022).

Previously, retrieval and LMs have been studied mostly separately, and only recently researchers have integrated them and built systems in which retrieval and LMs interact more organically, and a number of retrieval-based LMs have been proposed due to growing interest. They differ in their neural architectures (e.g., the granularity of retrieval units, how to integrate retrieved information), learning algorithms, and different uses in downstream applications. In this tutorial, we aim to provide a comprehensive and coherent overview of recent advances in retrieval-based LMs. We will start by first providing preliminaries covering the foundations of LM (e.g., masked LMs, autoregressive LMs) and retrieval systems (e.g., nearest-neighbor search methods widely used in neural retrieval systems; Karpukhin et al. 2020). We will then focus on recent progress in *architectures*, *learning approaches*, and *applications* of retrieval-based LMs.

A taxonomy of architectures We introduce a taxonomy of architectures of retrieval-based LMs based on a variety of dimensions. Retrieval-based LMs can be categorized by the granularity of retrieved units stored in the datastore: either 1) a chunk of text (Borgeaud et al., 2022; Izacard et al., 2022b), or 2) a token (Khandelwal et al., 2020; Zhong et al., 2022; Min et al., 2022), or 3) an entity mention (Févry et al., 2020; de Jong et al., 2022). We also plan to cover techniques for refining data stores and improving similarity search (He et al., 2021; Alon et al., 2022). At the same time, retrieval-base LMs can be categorized based on how the retrieved information is integrated with the parametric encoder: 1) whether retrieved components are concatenated with the original input text (Lewis et al., 2020; Guu et al., 2020; Izacard et al., 2022b), 2) whether the retrieved components are latent and integrated into the intermediate layers of Transformers (de Jong et al., 2022; Févry et al., 2020; Borgeaud et al., 2022), or 3) distribution of tokens from the retrieved components and the LMs are interpolated (Khandelwal et al., 2020; Zhong et al., 2022; Yogatama et al., 2021).

Scalable learning algorithms Then, we discuss the *training approaches* of retrieval-based LMs. Since a retrieval datastore is typically very large, how to train retrieval-based LMs effectively and efficiently remains challenging. We first discuss pipelined approaches that train retrieval components and LMs separately, either through large-

Proceedings of the 61st Annual Meeting of the Association for Computational Linguistics
Volume 6: Tutorial Abstracts, pages 41–46
July 9, 2023 ©2023 Association for Computational Linguistics

scale pre-training (Izacard et al., 2022a) or multi-task instruction tuning (Asai et al., 2022). Several other works train retrieval-based LMs with a fixed retrieval module (Borgeaud et al., 2022; Yogatama et al., 2021). We then discuss joint training under reasonable resource requirements: either through in-batch approximations to a full datastore, or updating the datastore with updated parameters asynchronously. The former uses fractions of the full corpus that are carefully designed during joint training (Zhong et al., 2022; de Jong et al., 2022; Min et al., 2022). The latter, on the other hand, aims to use full corpus during training with asynchronous index update for every certain time steps (Izacard et al., 2022b; Guu et al., 2020).

Adaption to downstream tasks After discussing the basic building blocks of retrieval-based LMs, we show how retrieval-based LMs are adapted to downstream applications. We first briefly summarize the two approaches to adapt a model to a new task: zero-shot or few-shot prompting without any parameter updates (Shi et al., 2022; Wang et al., 2022), and fine-tuning on target task data (Lewis et al., 2020). We then discuss methods designed to build more powerful retrieval-based LMs for certain downstream tasks, such as dialogue (Shuster et al., 2021), semantic parsing (Pasupat et al., 2021), and machine translation (Khandelwal et al., 2021; Zheng et al., 2021).

Up to this point, our tutorial has mainly focused on retrieving and integrating English plain text. At this end, we will cover recent extensions of retrieval-based LMs beyond English text, including multilingual (Asai et al., 2021), multimodal (Chen et al., 2022; Yasunaga et al., 2022) and code (Parvez et al., 2021) retrieval. These works often extend dense retrieval models to enable retrieval between heterogeneous input spaces (e.g., cross-lingual, cross-modal) and have shown that referring retrieved knowledge leads to knowledge-intensive generation.

Finally, we will use an exercise to showcase the effectiveness of retrieval-based LMs. We conclude our tutorial by discussing several important questions and future directions, including (1) how we can further improve the scalability of retrieval-based LMs without sacrificing performance, (2) when retrieval-based LMs are particularly useful in the era of rapidly evolving LMs, and (3) what is necessary to enable applications of retrieval-based LMs for more diverse domains.

2 Tutorial Outline

1. Introduction (15 minutes)

- An overview of the tutorial
- Why retrieval-based LMs?

2. Preliminaries (15 minutes)

- Language models: Auto-regressive LMs vs. masked LMs
- Dense retrieval methods
- Approximate nearest neighbor search

3. Retrieval-based LMs: A taxonomy of architectures (40 minutes)

- Granularity of datastore: tokens, entity mentions, and chunks of text
- How retrieved information is integrated: incorporation in the input layer, intermediate layers, and the output layer

4. Retrieval-based LMs: Scalable learning algorithms (40 minutes)

- Pipelined training
- Training with In-batch approximations
- Joint training of retrieval and LMs with asynchronous updates of corpus

5. Retrieval-based LMs: Downstream adaptations (40 minutes)

- Adaptation methods: zero-shot/few-shot prompting and fine-tuning on downstream tasks
- Downstream applications and task-specific modifications (e.g., dialogue, semantic parsing)

6. Extensions beyond English text (10 minutes)

- Multilingual retrieval-based LMs
- Multimodal retrieval-based LMs
- Code generation

7. Demostration: An exercise to show retrieval-augmented LMs (10 minutes)

8. Conclusions and future directions (10 minutes)

3 Tutorial Information

Type of the tutorial Cutting-edge.

Length This is a 3-hour tutorial.

Target audience The tutorial will be accessible to anyone who has a basic knowledge of machine learning and natural language processing. We think the topic will be of interest to both NLP researchers/students in academia and NLP practitioners in the industry.

Breadth We estimate that 20% of the work covered in this tutorial will be by the presenters and the remaining 80% by others. The papers we will cover are from both academia and industry.

Diversity considerations. The speakers are from two academic institutions with an affiliation with an industry research group, including both a professor and Ph.D. students. Three out of four speakers are female. The methods covered by our tutorials can scale up to various languages or domains, and we also briefly cover several papers focusing on multilingual and expert-domain extensions of the core frameworks. We will reach out to academic communities such as WiNLP[1] and Masakhane[2] to encourage them to attend our tutorial for participation of diverse audiences. Since retrieval-based LMs are alternatives to LMs with a significantly large number of parameters, we expect this tutorial to be especially useful to researchers with modest resources who do no have access to very large models.

An estimate of the audience size Given that language models are now used in a range of NLP tasks and retrieval-based approaches have been applied to diverse domains, we estimate that the number of audiences will be around 150+.

Venues. We prefer ACL due to the growing interest in the area and the travel constraints of some of the speakers. EMNLP is our second preferred choice, and we currently do not consider EACL.

Technical equipment. We would like to have Internet access to show online demos.

Open access We plan to make all teaching material available online and agree to allow the publication of slides and video recordings in the ACL anthology.

[1] http://www.winlp.org/

[2] https://www.masakhane.io/

Ethical considerations Retrieval-based LMs are often more powerful and parameter-efficient than LMs, and do not require full re-training to update world knowledge, which makes it more energy-efficient and can reduce carbon footprints. Prior work also shows that referring to external world knowledge can reduce harmful biases and hallucinations, although retrieval-based LMs can still be plausible sounding but incorrect or non-sensical outputs. We note that, as retrieval-based LMs may retrieve raw data from a corpus, which can leak privacy-sensitive information, especially when they are built on top of a private corpus. We acknowledge this to caution those who manage to apply retrieval-based LMs to privacy-sensitive domains.

Pedagogical material We plan to do some short hands-on exercises to let the audience try different retrieval-based LMs with few-shot prompting using Colab.

Past tutorials.

- ACL 2020 tutorial on Open-domain QA (Chen and Yih, 2020): This tutorial provides comprehensive reviews of open-domain question answering, some of which consist of a retriever and a generative model, while we focus on the recent progress of architectures and learning algorithms of retrieval-based LMs for diverse NLP tasks, not limiting its focus to open-domain QA. Most of the papers will be discussed in this tutorial have been published since the Open-domain QA tutorial three years ago. Moreover, one of the instructors, Danqi was an instructor of this ACL 2020 tutorial.

- SIGIR 2022 tutorial on Recent Advances in Retrieval-Augmented Text Generation (Cai et al., 2022): This tutorial focuses mainly on recent retrieval-augmented text generation approaches with a focus on two applications: dialogue and machine translation. Our tutorial puts more emphasis on the architecture and learning methods of retrieval-based LMs that can be applicable to diverse NLP tasks.

4 Presenters

Akari Asai Akari Asai is a Ph.D. student in the Paul G. Allen School of Computer Science & Engineering at the University of Washington, advised by Prof. Hannaneh Hajishirzi. Her research lies in natural language processing and machine learning. Her recent research focuses on question answering, retrieval-based LMs, multilingual NLP, and entity-aware representations. She received the IBM Fellowship in 2022. She is a lead organizer of the Workshop on Multilingual Information Access (NAACL 2022) and serves as an area chair in question answering at EACL 2023.

Sewon Min Sewon Min is a Ph.D. student in the Paul G. Allen School of Computer Science & Engineering at the University of Washington, and a visiting researcher at Meta AI. Her research spans question answering, representation and retrieval of factoid knowledge, and language modeling. She was a co-instructor and a co-organizer of multiple tutorials and workshops at ACL, NAACL-HLT, EMNLP, NeurIPS and AKBC, including a tutorial on Few-Shot NLP with Pretrained Language Models (ACL 2022), a tutorial on NLP for Long Sequences (NAACL-HLT 2021), and the Workshop on Semiparametric Methods in NLP (ACL 2022).

Zexuan Zhong Zexuan Zhong is a Ph.D. student in the Department of Computer Science at Princeton University, advised by Prof. Danqi Chen. His research interests lie in natural language processing and machine learning. His recent research focuses on retrieval-based LMs, generalization of retrieval models, and efficient models in NLP. He received a J.P. Morgan PhD Fellowship in 2022.

Danqi Chen Danqi Chen is an Assistant Professor of Computer Science at Princeton University and co-leads the Princeton NLP Group. Her recent research focuses on training, adapting, and understanding large LMs, and developing scalable and generalizable NLP systems for question answering, information extraction, and conversational agents. Danqi is a recipient of a Sloan Fellowship, a Samsung AI Researcher of the Year award, outstanding paper awards from ACL 2016, EMNLP 2017 and ACL 2022, and multiple industry faculty awards. Danqi served as the program chair for AKBC 2021 and (senior) area chairs for many *ACL conferences. She taught a tutorial on "Open-domain Question Answering" at ACL 2020.

5 Reading List

- Unsupervised Dense Information Retrieval with Contrastive Learning (Izacard et al., 2022a)
- Task-aware Retrieval with Instructions (Asai et al., 2022)
- Atlas: Few-shot Learning with Retrieval Augmented Language Models (Izacard et al., 2022b)
- Improving language models by retrieving from trillions of tokens (Borgeaud et al., 2022)
- Mention Memory: incorporating textual knowledge into Transformers through entity mention attention (de Jong et al., 2022)
- Generalization through Memorization: Nearest Neighbor Language Models (Khandelwal et al., 2020)
- Nonparametric Masked Language Model (Min et al., 2022)
- Training Language Models with Memory Augmentation (Zhong et al., 2022)
- kNN-Prompt: Nearest Neighbor Zero-Shot Inference (Shi et al., 2022)
- Neuro-Symbolic Language Modeling with Automaton-augmented Retrieval (Alon et al., 2022)

References

Uri Alon, Frank F. Xu, Junxian He, Sudipta Sengupta, Dan Roth, and Graham Neubig. 2022. Neuro-symbolic language modeling with automaton-augmented retrieval. In *International Conference on Machine Learning (ICML)*, Baltimore, USA.

Akari Asai, Timo Schick, Patrick Lewis, Xilun Chen, Gautier Izacard, Sebastian Riedel, Hannaneh Hajishirzi, and Wen-tau Yih. 2022. Task-aware retrieval with instructions. *arXiv preprint arXiv:2211.09260.*

Akari Asai, Xinyan Yu, Jungo Kasai, and Hanna Hajishirzi. 2021. One question answering model for many languages with cross-lingual dense passage retrieval. In *Advances in Neural Information Processing Systems.*

Bernd Bohnet, Vinh Q Tran, Pat Verga, Roee Aharoni, Daniel Andor, Livio Baldini Soares, Jacob Eisenstein, Kuzman Ganchev, Jonathan Herzig, Kai Hui, et al. 2022. Attributed question answering: Evaluation and modeling for attributed large language models. *arXiv preprint arXiv:2212.08037.*

Sebastian Borgeaud, Arthur Mensch, Jordan Hoffmann, Trevor Cai, Eliza Rutherford, Katie Millican, George Bm Van Den Driessche, Jean-Baptiste Lespiau, Bogdan Damoc, Aidan Clark, Diego De Las Casas, Aurelia Guy, Jacob Menick, Roman Ring, Tom Hennigan, Saffron Huang, Loren Maggiore, Chris Jones, Albin Cassirer, Andy Brock, Michela Paganini, Geoffrey Irving, Oriol Vinyals, Simon Osindero, Karen Simonyan, Jack Rae, Erich Elsen, and Laurent Sifre. 2022. Improving language models by retrieving from trillions of tokens. In *Proceedings of the 39th International Conference on Machine Learning*.

Tom Brown, Benjamin Mann, Nick Ryder, Melanie Subbiah, Jared D Kaplan, Prafulla Dhariwal, Arvind Neelakantan, Pranav Shyam, Girish Sastry, Amanda Askell, et al. 2020. Language models are few-shot learners. In *Advances in neural information processing systems*.

Deng Cai, Yan Wang, Lemao Liu, and Shuming Shi. 2022. Recent advances in retrieval-augmented text generation. In *Proceedings of the 45th International ACM SIGIR Conference on Research and Development in Information Retrieval*.

Nicholas Carlini, Florian Tramer, Eric Wallace, Matthew Jagielski, Ariel Herbert-Voss, Katherine Lee, Adam Roberts, Tom Brown, Dawn Song, Ulfar Erlingsson, et al. 2021. Extracting training data from large language models. In *30th USENIX Security Symposium (USENIX Security 21)*.

Danqi Chen and Wen-tau Yih. 2020. Open-domain question answering. In *Proceedings of the 58th Annual Meeting of the Association for Computational Linguistics: Tutorial Abstracts*, pages 34–37, Online. Association for Computational Linguistics.

Wenhu Chen, Hexiang Hu, Xi Chen, Pat Verga, and William W Cohen. 2022. Murag: Multimodal retrieval-augmented generator for open question answering over images and text. In *Proceedings of the 2021 Conference on Empirical Methods in Natural Language Processing*.

Aakanksha Chowdhery, Sharan Narang, Jacob Devlin, Maarten Bosma, Gaurav Mishra, Adam Roberts, Paul Barham, Hyung Won Chung, Charles Sutton, Sebastian Gehrmann, et al. 2022. PaLM: Scaling language modeling with pathways. *arXiv preprint arXiv:2204.02311*.

Nicola De Cao, Wilker Aziz, and Ivan Titov. 2021. Editing factual knowledge in language models. In *Proceedings of the 2021 Conference on Empirical Methods in Natural Language Processing*.

Michiel de Jong, Yury Zemlyanskiy, Nicholas FitzGerald, Fei Sha, and William W. Cohen. 2022. Mention memory: incorporating textual knowledge into transformers through entity mention attention. In *International Conference on Learning Representations*.

Thibault Févry, Livio Baldini Soares, Nicholas FitzGerald, Eunsol Choi, and Tom Kwiatkowski. 2020. Entities as experts: Sparse memory access with entity supervision. In *Proceedings of the 2020 Conference on Empirical Methods in Natural Language Processing*.

Kelvin Guu, Kenton Lee, Zora Tung, Panupong Pasupat, and Mingwei Chang. 2020. Retrieval augmented language model pre-training. In *International Conference on Machine Learning*.

Junxian He, Graham Neubig, and Taylor Berg-Kirkpatrick. 2021. Efficient nearest neighbor language models. In *Proceedings of the 2021 Conference on Empirical Methods in Natural Language Processing*, Punta Cana, Dominican Republic.

Gautier Izacard, Mathilde Caron, Lucas Hosseini, Sebastian Riedel, Piotr Bojanowski, Armand Joulin, and Edouard Grave. 2022a. Unsupervised dense information retrieval with contrastive learning. *Transactions on Machine Learning Research*.

Gautier Izacard, Patrick Lewis, Maria Lomeli, Lucas Hosseini, Fabio Petroni, Timo Schick, Jane Dwivedi-Yu, Armand Joulin, Sebastian Riedel, and Edouard Grave. 2022b. Few-shot learning with retrieval augmented language models. *arXiv preprint arXiv:2208.03299*.

Nikhil Kandpal, Haikang Deng, Adam Roberts, Eric Wallace, and Colin Raffel. 2022. Large language models struggle to learn long-tail knowledge. *arXiv preprint arXiv:2211.08411*.

Vladimir Karpukhin, Barlas Oguz, Sewon Min, Patrick Lewis, Ledell Wu, Sergey Edunov, Danqi Chen, and Wen-tau Yih. 2020. Dense passage retrieval for open-domain question answering. In *Proceedings of the 2020 Conference on Empirical Methods in Natural Language Processing (EMNLP)*, pages 6769–6781, Online. Association for Computational Linguistics.

Jungo Kasai, Keisuke Sakaguchi, Yoichi Takahashi, Ronan Le Bras, Akari Asai, Xinyan Yu, Dragomir Radev, Noah A Smith, Yejin Choi, and Kentaro Inui. 2022. Realtime qa: What's the answer right now? *arXiv preprint arXiv:2207.13332*.

Urvashi Khandelwal, Angela Fan, Dan Jurafsky, Luke Zettlemoyer, and Mike Lewis. 2021. Nearest neighbor machine translation. In *International Conference on Learning Representations*.

Urvashi Khandelwal, Omer Levy, Dan Jurafsky, Luke Zettlemoyer, and Mike Lewis. 2020. Generalization through memorization: Nearest neighbor language models. In *International Conference on Learning Representations*.

Angeliki Lazaridou, Adhi Kuncoro, Elena Gribovskaya, Devang Agrawal, Adam Liska, Tayfun Terzi, Mai Gimenez, Cyprien de Masson d'Autume, Tomas Kocisky, Sebastian Ruder, et al. 2021. Mind the gap: Assessing temporal generalization in neural language models. *Advances in Neural Information Processing Systems*.

Patrick Lewis, Ethan Perez, Aleksandra Piktus, Fabio Petroni, Vladimir Karpukhin, Naman Goyal, Heinrich Küttler, Mike Lewis, Wen-tau Yih, Tim Rocktäschel, Sebastian Riedel, and Douwe Kiela. 2020. Retrieval-augmented generation for knowledge-intensive nlp tasks. In *Advances in Neural Information Processing Systems*.

Alex Mallen, Akari Asai, Victor Zhong, Rajarshi Das, Hannaneh Hajishirzi, and Daniel Khashabi. 2022. When not to trust language models: Investigating effectiveness and limitations of parametric and non-parametric memories. *arXiv preprint arXiv:2212.10511*.

Jacob Menick, Maja Trebacz, Vladimir Mikulik, John Aslanides, Francis Song, Martin Chadwick, Mia Glaese, Susannah Young, Lucy Campbell-Gillingham, Geoffrey Irving, et al. 2022. Teaching language models to support answers with verified quotes. *arXiv preprint arXiv:2203.11147*.

Sewon Min, Weijia Shi, Mike Lewis, Xilun Chen, Wen-tau Yih, Hannaneh Hajishirzi, and Luke Zettlemoyer. 2022. Nonparametric masked language modeling. *arXiv preprint arXiv:2212.01349*.

Md Rizwan Parvez, Wasi Ahmad, Saikat Chakraborty, Baishakhi Ray, and Kai-Wei Chang. 2021. Retrieval augmented code generation and summarization. In *Findings of the Association for Computational Linguistics: EMNLP 2021*, pages 2719–2734, Punta Cana, Dominican Republic. Association for Computational Linguistics.

Panupong Pasupat, Yuan Zhang, and Kelvin Guu. 2021. Controllable semantic parsing via retrieval augmentation. In *Proceedings of the 2021 Conference on Empirical Methods in Natural Language Processing*.

Adam Roberts, Colin Raffel, and Noam Shazeer. 2020. How much knowledge can you pack into the parameters of a language model? In *Proceedings of the 2020 Conference on Empirical Methods in Natural Language Processing*.

Weijia Shi, Julian Michael, Suchin Gururangan, and Luke Zettlemoyer. 2022. Nearest neighbor zero-shot inference. In *Proceedings of the 2021 Conference on Empirical Methods in Natural Language Processing*.

Kurt Shuster, Spencer Poff, Moya Chen, Douwe Kiela, and Jason Weston. 2021. Retrieval augmentation reduces hallucination in conversation. In *Findings of the Association for Computational Linguistics: EMNLP 2021*.

Zhenhailong Wang, Xiaoman Pan, Dian Yu, Dong Yu, Jianshu Chen, and Heng Ji. 2022. Zemi: Learning zero-shot semi-parametric language models from multiple tasks. *arXiv preprint arXiv:2210.00185*.

Michihiro Yasunaga, Armen Aghajanyan, Weijia Shi, Rich James, Jure Leskovec, Percy Liang, Mike Lewis, Luke Zettlemoyer, and Wen-tau Yih. 2022. Retrieval-augmented multimodal language modeling. *arXiv preprint arXiv:2211.12561*.

Dani Yogatama, Cyprien de Masson d'Autume, and Lingpeng Kong. 2021. Adaptive semiparametric language models. *Transactions of the Association for Computational Linguistics*, 9:362–373.

Xin Zheng, Zhirui Zhang, Junliang Guo, Shujian Huang, Boxing Chen, Weihua Luo, and Jiajun Chen. 2021. Adaptive nearest neighbor machine translation. In *Proceedings of the 59th Annual Meeting of the Association for Computational Linguistics and the 11th International Joint Conference on Natural Language Processing*.

Zexuan Zhong, Tao Lei, and Danqi Chen. 2022. Training language models with memory augmentation. In *Proceedings of the 2021 Conference on Empirical Methods in Natural Language Processing*.

Author Index